The Role of Information and
Communication Technologies in
Postconflict Reconstruction

A WORLD BANK STUDY

The Role of Information and Communication Technologies in Postconflict Reconstruction

THE WORLD BANK
Washington, D.C.

Contents

PART-II

Boxes

Figures

Map

The Role of Information and Communication Technologies in Postconflict Reconstruction
http://dx.doi.org/10.1596/978-1-4648-0074-0

Acknowledgments

This report, on the role of *Information and Communication Technologies in Postconflict Reconstruction*, was commissioned by *info*Dev, a Global Partnership Program within the World Bank Group (www.infodev.org). The main report was written and the case study chapters edited by Dr. David Souter, *ict* Development Associates. The case study chapters represented here are summaries of much longer research projects carried out in 2012–13, which are available at www.infodev.org/postconflict. The Afghanistan case study, and accompanying video, was carried out by Dr. Siddhartha Raja, ICT Policy Specialist, World Bank. The Liberia case study was carried out by Dr. Michael Best, associate professor of the Georgia Institute of Technology. The Rwanda Case study was carried out by Mr. Nicolas Friederici, Oxford Internet Institute, with inputs from Mr. Kevin Donovan, University of Cape Town, and Mr Abdighani Jama, Somali Telecom Operators Association. The Timor-Leste case study was carried out by Dr. Chanuka Wattegama, LIRNEasia. The Tunisia case study was conducted by Mr. Zach Brisson and Ms. Kate Krontiris, of the social impact consultancy, Reboot.

The overall program was led by Dr Tim Kelly, Lead ICT Policy Specialist, assisted by Mr. Nicolas Friederici, Mr. Kevin Donovan, and Ms. Akshaya Sreenivasan, Penn State University. The program was generously financed by UKaid. Each of the individual chapters was separately peer reviewed by teams of national and international experts. The overall report was reviewed, and approved for publication, at a meeting on 12 June 2013, chaired by Ms. Samia Melhem, Lead ICT Policy Specialist, World Bank. The peer reviewers for the study were Ms. Amela Odobasic, Head of Public Affairs of the Communications Regulatory Agency of Bosnia and Herzegovina, Mr. Daniel Stauffacher and Ms. Simone Eymann of the ICT for Peace Foundation, Dr. Boutheina Guermazi, Senior Regulatory Specialist, World Bank, Mr. Erik Johnson, Senior Operations Officer, World Bank, and Ms. Sarah Cliffe, Special Advisor, World Bank. The World Bank team would like to thank all of those who contributed to this report.

About the Authors

Dr. Tim Kelly is a lead ICT policy specialist in the ICT Sector Unit of the World Bank Group, which he joined in 2008, initially to work with *info*Dev. He manages the analytical work program on ICT for Development, which, in 2012, saw the publication of the flagship reports on *Mobilizing Mobile* and *eTransform Africa*. On the operational side, he is currently managing ICT sector support programs in Botswana, Comoros, Mauritius, South Sudan, and Somalia. He was formerly head of the Strategy and Policy Unit of the International Telecommunication Union (ITU), and previously worked with the OECD and Logica Consultancy Ltd.

Over the last 25 years, Dr. Kelly has specialized in the economics of information and communication technologies. He has written or coauthored more than 30 books on the subject, including the World Bank's *Broadband Strategies Handbook*, ITU's *Internet Reports* and *World Telecommunication Development Report*, and OECD's *Communications Outlook*. He has an MA (Hons) degree in geography and a PhD in industrial economics from Cambridge University.

Dr. David Souter is an independent expert in ICT policy and regulation and in the interface between ICTs and public policy issues including development, environment, governance, and rights. He is managing director of the consultancy *ict* Development Associates, which he formed in 2003. He is visiting professor in communications management at the University of Strathclyde and visiting senior fellow in the Department of Media and Communications at the London School of Economics and Political Science. He is also president of the Global Connectivity Group for Sustainable Development. From 1995 to 2003 he was chief executive of the Commonwealth Telecommunications Organization. He was educated at the Universities of Cambridge and Oxford.

Abbreviations

ACE	African Coast to Europe, submarine cable
AIDS	acquired immunodeficiency syndrome
ANC	Autoridade Nacional de Communicações, Timor-Leste
ARCOM	Autoridade Reguladora das Communicações, Timor-Leste
ART	antiretroviral therapy
ATRA	Afghan Telecommunications Regulatory Authority
BPO	business process outsourcing
CCL	Cable Consortium of Liberia
EASSY	East African Submarine System, submarine cable
EDGE	Enhanced Data rates for GSM Evolution
EVC+	E-voucher Communications, service offered by Hormuud Telecom, Somalia
EWS	early warning systems
FM	frequency modulation
GDP	gross domestic product
Georgia Tech	Georgia Institute of Technology
GIS	geographic information systems
GNI	gross national income
GONU	Government of National Unity
GOSS	Government of Southern Sudan
GPRS	General Packet Radio Service
GSM	Global System for Mobile communications
HIV	human immunodeficiency virus
ICT	information and communication technologies
ICT4D	information and communication technologies for development
IGO	intergovernmental organization
IM	instant messenger
ISP	Internet service provider
ITES	ICT-enabled services

ITU	International Telecommunication Union
IXP	Internet exchange point
KIST	Kigali Institute of Science & Technology
KOICA	Korea International Cooperation Agency
LDC	least developed countries
LTA	Liberia Telecommunications Authority
Mbps	megabits per second
MCIT	Ministry of Communications and Information Technology, Afghanistan
MDG	Millennium Development Goals
NICI	National Information and Communication Infrastructure
NITC	National Information Technology Commission, Rwanda
NGO	nongovernmental organization
OLPC	One Laptop Per Child
PC	personal computer
PMIS	Personnel Management Information System
PPIAF	Public-Private Infrastructure Advisory Facility
RCIP	Regional Communications Infrastructure Programme
RITA	Rwandan Information Technology Authority
ROSS	Republic of South Sudan
RURA	Rwandan Utilities Regulatory Authority
SIDA	Swedish International Development Cooperation Agency
SIM	Subscriber Identity Module
SME	small and medium-sized enterprises
SMS	short message service
TRC	Truth and Reconciliation Commission
UNDP	United Nations Development Programme
USAID	United States Agency for International Development
USSD	unstructured supplementary service data
VCN	Village Communications Network, Afghanistan
VSAT	very small aperture terminal
WARCIP	West African Regional Communications Infrastructure Program
WBG	World Bank Group
W-CDMA	Wideband Code Division Multiple Access

PART I

An Overview and Framework for Analysis

Introduction

This report is concerned with the relationship between information and communication technologies (ICTs) and postconflict reconstruction, especially with ways in which ICTs can be used by governments and donors to support the transition from violence to stability.

The World Bank Group (WBG) has been concerned with sustainable recovery from violent conflict since its origins in 1944—as the name of its leading institution, the International Bank for Reconstruction and Development, indicates. It reviewed experience in postconflict reconstruction at the end of the 1990s[1] and, more recently, in its 2011 *World Development* Report.[2] Development, the WBG recognizes, cannot be achieved in a context of violence and instability. Reconstruction, reconciliation, and the achievement of sustainable, stable government are crucial to economic growth, poverty reduction, and social welfare in countries that have experienced international or civil war. The role of ICTs in development has also been prominent within the Bank's portfolio since the 1990s, as they have developed rapidly in technological complexity and geographic reach, becoming ever more central to government and business, to the sharing of knowledge, and to interactions between individuals and within communities.[3]

This opening chapter of the report gives an overview of the relationship between conflict, reconstruction and the role of ICTs. It builds on experience within the Bank as well as on a wide range of practitioner, academic, and other literature. It draws on five case studies of aspects of ICT development in societies emerging from conflict, which were commissioned by the Bank and which are reported in subsequent chapters. These case studies were specifically chosen to reflect the experiences of widely differing countries, at different stages of recovery from conflict: Afghanistan following decades of civil war followed by international intervention; Liberia following a negotiated settlement to protracted civil war; Timor-Leste since its troubled acquisition of independence; Rwanda seeking stability in the aftermath of genocide; and Tunisia, which recently experienced not civil war but insurrection leading to a change of government. Two boxes also draw attention to developments in postconflict countries where the World Bank is currently undertaking work concerned with ICTs, the Republic of Somalia and the Republic of South Sudan.

The overview in this chapter seeks to establish a framework for understanding the ways in which ICTs interact with societies in transition from violence to stability, and for leveraging their potential to further that transition. The roots of this lie in understanding two fields of study, policy, and practice:

- Analysis of conflict and postconflict reconstruction
- Analysis of ICTs and the development of an information society.

These two fields are reviewed in Chapters 1 and 2. The third chapter then analyses the relationship between them and proposes a framework for analysis and policy development. Chapter 4 makes a number of recommendations to the World Bank Group, to other donors and development actors, as well as to the governments of countries emerging from violent conflict, and suggests areas for further research.

Notes

1. See Alcira Kreimer et al. (1998), "The World Bank's Experience with Post-Conflict Reconstruction," World Bank Operations Evaluation Department, available at http://lnweb90.worldbank.org/oed/oeddoclib.nsf/b57456d58aba40e585256ad400736404/f753e43e728a27b38525681700503796/$FILE/PostCon.pdf; World Bank (1998), "Post-Conflict Reconstruction: The Role of the World Bank," available at http://www-wds.worldbank.org/external/default/WDSContentServer/WDSP/IB/1998/04/01/000009265_3980624143531/Rendered/PDF/multi_page.pdf.

2. World Bank (2011), "World Development Report 2011: Conflict, Security and Development," available at http://web.worldbank.org/WBSITE/EXTERNAL/EXTDEC/EXTRESEARCH/EXTWDRS/0,,contentMDK:23252415~pagePK:478093~piPK:477627~theSitePK:477624,00.html.

3. The Bank's current strategy for ICT4D can be found in World Bank (2012), "ICT for Greater Development Impact," available at http://siteresources.worldbank.org/EXTINFORMATIONANDCOMMUNICATIONANDTECHNOLOGIES/Resources/WBG_ICT_Strategy-2012.pdf.

CHAPTER 1

Conflict, Reconstruction, and Development

It is important, in thinking about conflict, reconstruction, and development, to clarify the meaning of conflict and the challenges it poses. Conflict is, after all, as widely noted in the literature, central to human experience. People have always contested with one another for resources, power, and influence. Competition is at the heart of democratic elections and market economies. Conflict in most societies is mediated through institutions of governance and social norms. For this reason, some writers on conflict and stability emphasize that it is *violent* conflict rather than conflict *per se* that is the problem, and reject the term "post-conflict reconstruction," preferring to talk about social and political stabilization.[1] This chapter retains the term but recognizes its ambivalence.

The concept of "postconflict" reconstruction is closely connected with the broader concept of "fragile" statehood. States may be considered fragile for a wide variety of reasons other than conflict alone, including low levels of economic development, poor governance structures, vulnerability to natural disasters and food insecurity. In many cases, these causes of fragility are compounded by conflict. The Republic of Somalia, for instance, experienced a widespread drought just as it was emerging from a 20-year period of civil war. This is estimated to have killed more than a quarter of a million people between 2010 and 2012, while impoverishing many more.[2]

The focus of this report is on post*conflict* reconstruction, rather than the more widely studied field of post*disaster* recovery. Likewise, it concentrates on the role of information and communication technologies (ICTs) in *reconstruction* rather than their role in related fields such as peacekeeping and peacebuilding, on which there is already a substantial literature.[3] Conflicts—even those involving whole nations or large parts of them—vary greatly, but also share common characteristics and impacts. In recent years, conflicts between countries have become less frequent but civil conflicts have remained numerous, and now represent the majority of wars. Although largely contained within individual countries, these civil conflicts have spillover effects, especially within their regions but also more widely, including economic disruption, refugee absorption, epidemics, and terrorist activity. The report explores some aspects of the role of ICTs which are particularly prominent in these postconflict contexts, such as the need to rebuild infrastructure and the contribution of ICTs to truth and reconciliation processes.

Research undertaken for the World Bank in the early years of the last decade suggested that three factors are strongly associated with high levels of vulnerability to civil conflict. These three factors—low and declining *per capita* gross domestic product (GDP), poor income distribution, and a high degree of dependence on primary exports—are particularly characteristic of low-income developing countries, which suggests the importance of incorporating conflict and conflict risk into development models. Indeed, in their work for the Bank, Paul Collier and his colleagues described violent conflict as "development in reverse," calculating that economies grow more than 2 percent less *p.a.* in civil war than they would otherwise. In consequence, they argued, countries can become ensnared in a "conflict trap," illustrated by the frequency with which they may return to violence: there was, they said, a 44 percent chance of violent conflict returning to a country emerging from civil war within five years.[4]

Other factors—including ethnic, religious, and political rivalries—are also significant contributors to conflict risk in individual states. Fragile states are often characterized by weak government institutions, lack of social cohesion, weak, or absent civil society organizations, corrupt and unaccountable bureaucracies, and limited opportunities for ordinary citizens to participate in public life or influence decisions that affect their lives. These aspects of vulnerability to violent conflict are, like the economic factors identified above, also core development challenges.

While there are statistically identifiable common characteristics, however, it is equally important to recognize that conflicts differ significantly one from another, and there is no single common approach appropriate to all. While four of the five countries discussed in this volume have experienced violent civil conflict, there have been substantial differences among them: ethnic conflict in some but not all cases; international intervention in some but not all, sometimes by the United Nations, sometimes by other agencies; negotiated settlements in some, but not in others. The size and development characteristics of countries concerned are also variable: Timor-Leste, for example, is much smaller and more isolated than the other case study countries. Tunisia did not experience civil war but insurrection leading to the overthrow of a long-established and highly organized state apparatus. It serves as a reminder that conflicts do not all involve protracted violence or the destruction of infrastructure such as ICT facilities, and that contests for power can occur in countries with strong as well as weak governments. Conflict specialists emphasize the importance of understanding the particularities of individual conflicts, rather than making generalized assumptions about them.

As indicated above, the experience of international support demonstrates that strategies, tools, and means may not have the same effect on each postconflict environment. Nor do postconflict countries share a common timeline as they move toward stability, reconstruction, and development. Donors need to develop distinct strategic approaches which are tailored to the specific context and characteristics of each postconflict environment, taking into account the nature of the conflict concerned and of historical, economic, and cultural factors. The pace of implementation for strategic approaches is also crucial. Not all countries will be able to absorb and not all governments will be able to implement changes at the same pace; indeed, the pace of change itself is liable to change as a result of events and unexpected developments along the way. A long-term commitment to postconflict reconstruction, and flexibility, are therefore essential.

International intervention of some kind plays a part in the cessation of many conflicts, for example through United Nations or other peacekeeping forces.[5] Peace agreements, once they are in place, tend to lead (at least in developing countries) to rapid involvement by donors. Crisis mapping is often a first response to rebuilding, bringing in a number of different stakeholders.[6] Private sector investment generally takes longer, arriving when stability seems more assured, though mobile telecommunications has in recent years often been the first sector to experience substantial new investment.

1.1 A Framework for Understanding Postconflict Reconstruction

A number of terms are used for intervention at different phases in the transition from war to peace—peacekeeping, peacemaking, peacebuilding, and postconflict reconstruction, for example, the last of which is concerned with the development of a more stable security and political environment, which can generate the economic growth and social cohesion that are likely to contribute to sustainable peace. Confidence in a lasting peaceful settlement does not come quickly. As noted above, many conflicts recur; a decade or more may be needed before future prospects can be properly assessed. Donor support is often concentrated in the early years, but World Bank evidence suggests that it generally needs to last a decade, with most emphasis on the middle years as private investment begins to flow.[7]

Much has been written, by many commentators, about different aspects of peacebuilding and postconflict reconstruction. This literature cannot be reviewed at length here, but can be explored through some of the references in the reading list at the end of the report. Five themes, however, emerge from it as of critical importance, and provide a framework for the discussion of the potential contribution of ICTs later in this chapter. They are illustrated in figure 1.1.

- The first of these themes, **stabilization**, concerns the establishment of physical security and governmental institutions in whose integrity and viability both citizens and potential investors have confidence. Stability is an essential prerequisite for both reconstruction and development. Many things need to come together to achieve it, from demilitarization and the reintegration of former combatants and displaced persons to the establishment of competent and respected government and judicial institutions. Political processes which have the consent of all (or at least all major) parties are essential for stability:

The Role of Information and Communication Technologies in Postconflict Reconstruction
http://dx.doi.org/10.1596/978-1-4648-0074-0

Figure 1.1 A Framework for Understanding Postconflict Reconstruction

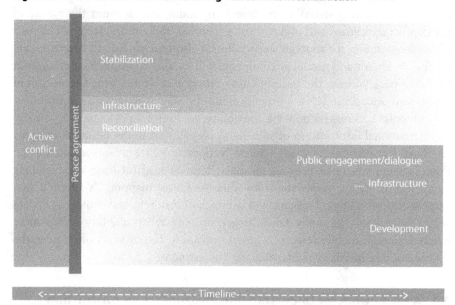

Source: World Bank data.

not simply elections but the checks and balances that are inherent to successful political systems and the inclusion of divided population groups. A return
to economic prosperity, creating employment and income-earning opportunities, will also make a powerful difference.[8]

- The second theme in this framework concerns the rebuilding of national **infrastructure**. Countries which have experienced civil war have usually seen
the destruction of physical infrastructures for power, communications, and
transport as well as social infrastructures such as those for health and education. The absence of infrastructure hinders reintegration and hamstrings development. Its restoration, on the other hand, builds faith in reconstruction
and recovery, and contributes fundamentally to the transition from stabilization to development. Infrastructure investment is capital intensive, however,
and requires time and planning, for both short and longer terms.

- The third theme is **reconciliation**. Violent conflicts involve complex webs of
perpetrators and victims. Civil wars inflict death, destruction, and assault on
civilian populations as well as—often more than—combatants. Communities
are divided within themselves and from one another. The task of building
mutual confidence, in particular confidence that violence will not recur, is
complex, difficult, and closely related to stabilization. One approach to reconciliation, used in some forty countries since it was pioneered in South Africa, has been the establishment of a Truth and Reconciliation Commission or
similar body, which seeks to overcome hostility by enabling all parties to explore the past together.[9] ICTs can also assist with the process of transitional
justice.

- The fourth theme, **public engagement**, concerns the involvement of citizens, businesses, and civil society organizations in the new polity that emerges from a peace agreement and reconstruction process. As well as being desirable for other reasons, public engagement is generally considered necessary in order to bring conflicts that could foster violence within political processes. Participation and inclusiveness should help to build cohesion in societies which have experienced repression and/or discrimination, such as that described in the Tunisian case study, as well as those that have experienced armed conflict. The contribution of participation and engagement to democracy and economic growth has been emphasized by the World Bank: ICTs can widen access to such public fora and can help promote diversity of voice, and protect anonymity, if required.[10] They are therefore associated with such processes as the introduction or reintroduction of electoral politics, and with issues of democracy and human rights. The development of new public spaces is not, however, without its dangers. Demagogues and hotheads can exploit the openness of public fora to undermine social cohesion and public order, at the expense of transparency and accountability.
- Fifthly and finally within this framework, reconstruction requires **development**. As noted earlier, societies whose economies are stagnant and in which social welfare is deteriorating are highly vulnerable to violent conflict or its resurgence. Armed conflict itself will almost certainly have undermined economic growth and destroyed economic assets and capabilities. Populations in conflict countries suffer from the flight of capital and skilled people, and the disruption of production and trade. They have ground to make up on their neighbors and competitors. ICT applications may contribute to reversing adverse capital flows following stabilization, particularly if remittances and other capital transfers can be made through mobile money. Equally, societies which experience growth, and in which the benefits of growth are reasonably well distributed, for example through increased employment, appear less vulnerable to conflict reemerging. Investment in development—by the international community and returning migrants—can therefore reinforce stability as it revitalizes economically.

While short- and medium-term reconstruction in postconflict countries includes priorities which are distinct from those of other developing nations, their long-term reconstruction aims merge over time into more conventional development objectives. Strategies for reconstruction need to look forward to development as well as looking sideways—building on stabilization, restoring infrastructure, facilitating reconciliation and encouraging the development of an inclusive and cohesive national polity.

The next chapter describes the impact of rapidly changing information and communication technology and markets on society, economy, politics, and culture—and in particular on social and economic development—during the past two decades. The implications and potentialities of ICTs and ICT-enabled services for the dimensions of reconstruction in the model discussed above are considered in the third chapter.

Notes

1. See for example, James Putzel and Jonathan Di John (2012), "Meeting the Challenges of Crisis States," London School of Economics Crisis Studies Research Centre.

2. FAO and FEWS Net (2013), "Mortality among Populations of Southern and Central Somalia, Affected by Severe Food Insecurity and Famine during 2010–2012," available at: http://www.fews.net/docs/Publications/Somalia_Mortality_Estimates_Final_Report_1May2013_upload.pdf.

3. See, for instance, the work of the ICT for Peace Foundation, notably Stauffacher et al (2005).

4. Paul Collier et al. (2003), *Breaking the Conflict Trap: Civil War and Development Policy*, World Bank Policy Research Report.

5. On UN peacekeeping, see United Nations (2008), "United Nations Peacekeeping Operations: Principles and Guidelines," available at http://pbpu.unlb.org/pbps/library/capstone_doctrine_eNg.pdf.

6. See ICT for Peace Foundation (2010), http://ict4peace.org/updates/report-of-the-un-secretary-general-underscores-crisis-information-management-strategy.

7. Cited in Paul Collier (2004), "Development and Conflict," Centre for the Study of African Economies, Oxford University, available at http://www.un.org/esa/documents/Development.and.Conflict2.pdf.

8. See for example, Roland Paris and Timothy D. Sisk (2008), "Introduction," In Paris & Sisk (eds), *The Dilemmas of Statebuilding: Confronting the Contradictions of Postwar Peace Operations*, Routledge.

9. For the South African Commission, see http://www.justice.gov.za/trc/.

10. See World Bank (2011), "World Development Report 2011: Conflict, Security and Development," World Bank.

CHAPTER 2

ICTs, Reconstruction, and Development

The information and communication technology (ICT) sector has been the most dynamic growth sector in the world economy over the past twenty years. Three ICTs, themselves increasingly convergent, have been particularly instrumental in the growth of what has become known as an Information Society.

- The spread and increasing sophistication of **computing** have transformed administration and business practice throughout the industrial world, and are doing so in larger and (increasingly) smaller organizations in developing countries. It has also transformed the lives and lifestyles of a growing number of individuals. Over a third of households worldwide are now estimated to have computers, including a quarter of those in developing countries.[1] Processes which would historically have been undertaken manually are now routinely performed by computers, which can collect, analyse, store, and share information in ways that were previously unfeasible. Together with the changes in information and communications described below, they have enabled new kinds of administration, different relationships between governments and citizens, and new ways of producing and distributing goods and services.
- The **Internet** and the World Wide Web have added enormously to the impact of computing by making it cheap and easy to share information between computer users anywhere. This has impacted on both information and communications. The Internet has lifted physical constraints on access to information: instead of relying on books, newspapers, or broadcast radio, anyone with an Internet connection can now access an extraordinarily diverse and comprehensive range of information—and opinion—from sources around the world, at the click of a mouse. It has established much simpler forms of rapid and instant communications, by email and instant messaging, which enable transfer of documents, audio, video, and other files between individuals and within groups in ways that were not previously possible. More recently, social networking and what are commonly called Web 2.0 services have enabled any user to publish online and made it far easier for social, political, and other groups to organize activities including participation in governance (and protests against governments).

- The third part of this convergent ICT triangle is **mobile telephony**. Fifteen years ago, telephones in developing countries were the preserve of governments, big businesses, and the very rich. Less than 1 percent of people in many countries had a phone. Today, there are almost as many mobile phone subscriptions as people in the world, and the majority of adults in the vast majority of countries are now connected.[2] Mobile phones are increasingly complex devices, offering users many complementary services as well as telephony. They are, in particular, the primary mode of Internet access and of access to social networking—in both personal and digital meanings of the term—for many people in developing countries. The ability of people to communicate at will with one another has had a transforming effect on their ability to access resources and to coordinate with one another,[3] one whose impact on political engagement was powerfully observed during the events of 2011/12 referred to as the Arab Spring.[4]

These three ICTs do not encompass everything about the developing Information Society, nor have they rendered earlier information and communication platforms—such as radio and television—redundant. They do, however, represent dramatic changes in the potential for information and communications in society. For most people in most countries, alone or together, they have expanded horizons, extended social contacts, and enabled empowerment. Governments and donors, nongovernmental organizations (NGOs), and businesses have used them to extend the reach and range of goods and services. The use of information and communications for development (ICT4D) has become increasingly prominent in the development strategies of governments, while individuals have proved adept at using mobile phones and the Internet to meet their own social, economic, and developmental needs. A wide range of applications have been developed to provide health and business information, training, financial services, and other resources of developmental value, and more such applications come into play each day. New ways of leveraging community knowledge and expertise such as crisis mapping and crowdsourcing, new ways of manipulating data, and new approaches to data transparency such as "open data" have added to the mix of resources available to governments, businesses, civil society organizations, and individuals.

The Information Society is not, of course, entirely benign. ICTs enhance the ability of people to do whatever it is they wish to do. While governments can use them to improve administration, deliver services, and empower citizens, they can also use them to manage information, monitor behavior, and control dissent. The Internet and other ICTs are valued by criminals and terrorists as well as citizens and governments. The platforms they provide for information and communications are used by warmongers as well as peacebrokers. As we consider ways in which ICTs can contribute to postconflict reconstruction, we should not forget that they can also be used to trigger or prolong conflict, as broadcast radio was used in Rwanda in the run-up to that country's 1994 genocide. Mitigating threats should be part of postconflict strategies for ICTs, as well as maximizing value.

The Role of Information and Communication Technologies in Postconflict Reconstruction
http://dx.doi.org/10.1596/978-1-4648-0074-0

What are the underlying requirements for ICTs to make a positive contribution to reconstruction and development? Evidence from postconflict and other developing countries clearly identifies four factors of particular importance—factors which are more interrelated than is sometimes recognized.

- Firstly, and most obviously, leveraging developmental value from communications requires **infrastructure**, including backbone and access infrastructure in-country and connectivity to international networks. The importance of access to fiber-optic cable, rather than reliance on satellites for international connectivity, has been clear from recent experience in East Africa and is raised by the case studies of Liberia and Timor-Leste in this report. Network reach into rural and remoter areas is important not just for development but also national cohesion. Broadband infrastructure is now regarded as the necessary standard for future international competitiveness.[5]
- Secondly, growth in network deployment, access, and services is best secured through an **enabling environment** that encourages private sector investment. In practice, international communications businesses have been keen to invest in developing markets, and have invested in postconflict markets more quickly than those in other infrastructure sectors, recognizing the potential for rapid returns on investment and responding to high levels of demand for communication services, especially among diaspora and refugee communities.[6] Evidence shows that propensity to invest is increased by legal frameworks which encourage competition and by regulatory regimes which afford predictability and reduced regulatory risk—both factors which are associated with stable government and which acknowledge the value of cooperation between government and the private sector. Unclear conditions relating to licenses can deter investment and can slow the development of applications, such as mobile money.
- Thirdly, the capacity of developing countries in general, including postconflict countries, to take advantage of communications opportunities depends substantially on **underlying social and economic factors**. ICTs alone cannot compensate for shortages of skills, from literacy to computer maintenance; for lack of capital to start and develop businesses; for lack of confidence in security and prospects for the future. Indeed the increasing role of ICTs can exacerbate the impact of such shortages and weaknesses on national development, increasing rather than reducing divides within society. Although more difficult to address in the short term, securing medium- to long-term social and economic gains from ICTs requires improvements to demand-side factors such as education and training, capital markets, and the environment for local business development.
- Fourthly, all of this suggests the need for the ICT sector to be integrated into governmentwide **strategic approaches** to social and economic development, poverty reduction, and/or postconflict reconstruction. Governments in many countries have developed national ICT strategies, though these have often been aspirational and not always been well integrated with other government

The Role of Information and Communication Technologies in Postconflict Reconstruction
http://dx.doi.org/10.1596/978-1-4648-0074-0

or donor agendas. The institutional framework for implementation is often weak, and the underlying communications environment—the adoption and use of ICTs by citizens—uncertain. Rwanda's experience with ICT strategies, described later in this volume, illustrates both the opportunities and challenges involved.

Even where these underlying requirements are addressed, substantial challenges remain in maximizing the developmental potential of ICTs, particularly in least developed countries (LDCs) and fragile states. Network deployment in rural areas is rarely comparable with that in urban areas. Power outages, infrastructure weaknesses and affordability challenges constrain the ability of those on the margins to take advantage of the opportunities that ICTs can offer. Uneven access to ICTs and the ability to make use of them will have an impact on structures of power and prosperity.

The impact of the changing ICT environment on postconflict societies is substantially rooted in their wider development experience. Low-income LDCs such as Liberia and Rwanda, unsurprisingly, have less highly developed communications infrastructures than middle-income countries such as Tunisia. Applications and services are generally more developed, more geographically widespread, more inclusive, and more widely used in countries with higher average incomes, educational attainments, and economic opportunities. As countries emerge from conflict, their communications legacies—past experience and development of the sector, and the extent to which infrastructure and services have survived the conflict period—set the starting point for reconstruction efforts. These cannot and should not be separate from wider development agendas.

The experience of conflict, however, has significantly affected how the ICT sector has developed in different countries, and so significantly shapes the developmental approach required looking forward. Communications infrastructure is often destroyed during violent conflict, as happened in the case study countries of Liberia and Timor-Leste, as well as in Somalia. Even where infrastructure has not been destroyed, networks are unlikely to have been extended into hazardous or rebel-controlled areas. Conflict discourages private investment, inhibits policy and regulatory reform, and curtails economic activity that would encourage the adoption of new services. In Liberia, for example, it heightened isolation from global ICT developments by preventing connectivity to Africa's new submarine networks. The cessation of conflict therefore often leaves the ICT sectors of postconflict countries underdeveloped in comparison with those of neighboring countries. This is an initial disadvantage in terms of reconstruction, but also an opportunity for new investors to implement the latest technologies and network architectures.

At the same time, conflict may have enabled some alternative ways of meeting demand for ICTs. The absence of government and prolonged conflict between warlords did not prevent entrepreneurs in Somalia from developing viable, unregulated mobile phone networks.[7] Information affecting security is particularly valuable in times of crisis, including conflict, and citizens and communities have sought and exploited whatever ways they can find to gain and share such vital knowledge. Social networking services have proved particularly useful to populations at risk, as well as to opposition activists, in countries such as Tunisia which have experienced insurrection rather than war. The legacy of conflict for ICT networks and services is not, therefore, entirely negative. It includes experiences and innovations which can prove valuable in reconstruction and peacebuilding.[8]

Notes

1. http://www.itu.int/en/ITU-D/Statistics/Documents/statistics/2012/ITU_Key_2006-2013_ICT_data.xls.
2. World Bank (2012), "Information and Communications for Development 2012: Maximizing Mobile," available at: www.worldbank.org/ict/IC4D2012.
3. See UNDP (2012).
4. Dubai School of Government, Arab Social Media Report, May 2011.
5. See Tim Kelly et al. (2009), "What Role Should Governments Play in Broadband Development?," available at http://www.oecd.org/ict/4d/43631862.pdf; and the work of the Broadband Commission for Digital Development, at http://www.broadbandcommission.org/.
6. Jordan Schwartz et al. (2004), "The Private Sector's Role in the Provision of Infrastructure in Post-Conflict Countries: Patterns and Policy Options," World Bank, available at http://siteresources.worldbank.org/INTCPR/214578-1111996036679/20618754/WP16_Web.pdf.
7. See, for example, Wall Street Journal, 11 May 2010, "Telecom Firms Thrive in Somalia Despite War, Shattered Economy," available at http://online.wsj.com/article/SB10001424052748704608104575220570113266984.html.
8. The Ushahidi crisis mapping software, for instance, was developed following postelection violence in Kenya in 2008 and has subsequently been widely used around the world (see www.ushahidi.com).

CHAPTER 3

ICTs and Postconflict Reconstruction

Chapter 1 of this report identified five main areas of reconstruction policy and practice, concerned with

1. Stabilization
2. Infrastructure
3. Reconciliation
4. Public engagement
5. Development.

This chapter looks in turn at how information and communication technologies (ICTs) can contribute to each of these, exploring ICTs' potential value in addressing common challenges in postconflict contexts, drawing on the experiences described in the case studies and elsewhere. Chapter 4, which follows, draws on this discussion to suggest priorities for policy and practice by governments, donors, and other stakeholders in peacebuilding and reconstruction.

Countries that emerge from violent conflict share some common characteristics, but the importance of contextual differences among them should be borne constantly in mind. Conflicts have different causes and leave different consequences; countries have different characteristics, cultures, and economies; citizens have different needs, desires, and responsibilities. Postconflict societies are vulnerable to a return to violence, and reconstruction efforts need to be sensitive to risk as well as opportunity.

As already noted, underlying communications environments also share some characteristics but differ widely alongside other aspects of society. Cultural norms can be as important in this context as infrastructure—whether within the family or in relations between the citizen and state. Those who have grown up in countries where information has been tightly controlled often have different assumptions from those who have grown up in more open societies (including donors and those returning from diasporas). In addition, the ICTs that are available are themselves experiencing rapid change. Most of the postconflict situations discussed in this report pre-date the development of mass market mobile telephony or social media. This should be borne in mind when considering what lessons they may have for postconflict societies today.

3.1 Stabilization

Stabilization is the first priority of peacebuilding and reconstruction. Almost half of countries emerging from civil conflict revert to violence within five years.[1] Renewed conflict may even focus on different disputes from prior conflict, as was the case in Timor-Leste in 2006. Politically unstable countries can experience repeated developmental disruption, like the Union of the Comores, which has seen more than 20 coups and attempted coups since 1975. If reconstruction is to be sustainable, and development to follow, then governments and other stakeholders must do all they can, with the support of donors, to prevent violence from re-emerging.

Conflict prevention is, therefore, an essential part of stabilization and postconflict reconstruction. In the short term, this focuses on operational challenges, keeping the peace between ex-combatants, resolving disputes over shared resources, challenging aggressive behavior and the actions of those determined to spoil the peace and so on. Longer-term conflict prevention addresses the drivers of conflict, including poverty, lack of employment and opportunity, inhabiting the transition between stabilization and development.[2]

Avoiding renewed conflict is far from easy and requires coordination between actors to whom it may not come naturally—between former combatants, between donor agencies with different priorities and between government and civil society, government and media, and development and security personnel. These actors need to build a common understanding of the complex and often rapidly changing environment around them. There may be frequent crises, which require careful management and give-and-take between security and development priorities. Lessons will be learnt from local practice, as much as from experience elsewhere.

ICTs are unlikely to be seen by either governments or international agencies as the most important factors in stabilization but they can play a significant part in helping to ensure it stays on track, and should be incorporated accordingly in governments' and donors' plans. There is a need to build understanding among decision makers of the potential value and limitations of ICTs at different stages of postconflict reconstruction. The ways in which ICTs contribute at this stage also prepare the ground for longer-term roles which they can play as reconstruction unfolds, consolidating the gains achieved through stabilization and building platforms that contribute to social and economic development. The following paragraphs draw attention to four areas of particular significance.

The **restoration of telecommunications** itself plays a part in building public confidence that a country is returning to normality. Even if prior network infrastructure has been destroyed, emergency wireless and satellite communications can be put in place quickly, facilitating security and the return of displaced people to their home communities. Permanent wireless networks can be brought into operation much more quickly than the fixed networks that would once have been required. This helps government and other agencies to coordinate relief and also enables individuals to rebuild social relationships that have been separated by conflict, within families and beyond, including relationships between home and diaspora communities. People who acquire mobile phones in the aftermath of violent conflict stress their particular value in terms of personal security—increasing their ability to assess and avoid risks associated with travel, and to seek help when it is needed.[3] Telephony, in short, helps to restore the bonds that make society work.

As well as rebuilding social relationships and intercommunal confidence, restored telecommunications provide a basis for the development of economic activity, local and nationwide. A revitalized communications sector also impacts on national revenues. Governments and citizens both benefit from investments made by communications businesses, from the fees paid for licences; from the jobs created in deploying networks and managing services; and from the taxes generated by company profits and, where these are imposed, the use of telecoms networks for both local and international calls. Telecommunications companies are among the largest businesses in most developing countries and contribute significantly to tax revenues, their contribution in postconflict countries growing as stabilization continues and networks expand.

Two further aspects of restored communications are important in the initial postconflict period, as society adjusts to peace, and in the early days of stabilization—the supply of accurate information, and monitoring to provide early warning of potential trouble. While particularly important in these early stages, both of these also have lasting value as reconstruction proceeds.

Reliable information is critical in times of violent conflict, when knowing what is happening can make the difference between life and death. Reliable information is also hard to find during conflict, trumped by propaganda and rumor in the absence of independent media and reliable telecommunications. This does not change overnight when an armistice is signed. Donors and international intervention forces have learnt, from bitter experience, the importance of communicating directly and effectively with frightened and uncertain populations—providing reliable information to the community through officially sponsored radio programming, news bureaux that liaise with other radio stations, and public information offices.[4] Civil society organizations can also play an important part in building trustworthy information networks, while some communities have begun to organize their own using mobile telephones and social network applications. Well-distributed reliable information can help to dispel rumor and build confidence in peacebuilding, even where negative forces seek to undermine this.

While information dissemination is valuable for building confidence in the future, information gathering is essential for addressing threats to peace as and when they arise. **Early warning systems** (EWS), which seek to identify where confrontations between former combatants (or other actors) threaten to break out into violence, are particularly important in the early days of peacebuilding, and remain important throughout the reconstruction period. Historically, they have relied on top-down intelligence gathering, using government officials and

The Role of Information and Communication Technologies in Postconflict Reconstruction
http://dx.doi.org/10.1596/978-1-4648-0074-0

military or security personnel, often from international intervention forces with little local experience.

New ICTs have now enabled what have become known as third- and fourth-generation early warning systems to leverage information from within communities themselves.[5] Official EWS and independent applications can both provide channels through which individuals are able to report incidents that threaten peace (as well as requirements for material relief), making use of both the general public and selected trusted individuals as informants. Information from crowdsourced applications of this kind can be combined with geographic mapping to coordinate security response and defuse threats before they jeopardize wider peace agreements.

The use of Ushahidi software to monitor violence during Kenya's postelection crisis during 2007/08 was a pioneering example of how this can be done, enabling interventions that reduced the risk of violence escalating and building a reputation for Ushahidi that led to its much wider use elsewhere.[6] ICTs were also deployed more officially in the 2013 elections in Kenya, though with mixed results.[7] Biometric voter identification failed on the day of the election, in some areas due to power failure. Electronic transmission of results, using short message service (SMS), also became overloaded, prompting accusations of vote-rigging, although a more likely explanation for this was inadequate testing in advance of use. However, the deployment of an adapted Ushahidi platform—Uchaguzi[8]—for monitoring and citizen reporting of violence during the 2013 elections seems to have worked well.

As in the past, however, early warning systems are only as useful as the response mechanisms which are in place to mitigate threats and avert return to violence once they are triggered. Experience in South Sudan has shown some positive results from crowdsourced and ICT-enabled early warning mechanisms, but also illustrated challenges—including deliberate misreporting of incidents in order to secure intervention or advantage as well as the need to integrate warning and response. A recent analysis in that country concludes that:

> Tech-enabled conflict-prevention initiatives work best when they enhance traditional conflict-prevention, early-warning, and early-response mechanisms, working with existing structures rather than enabling new ones,[9]

a conclusion that resonates with other aspects of postconflict work where ICTs are used to protect and promote peaceful outcomes.

Coordination is the fourth challenge that faces governments, donors, and international intervention forces in the early days of reconstruction, as they seek to bring stability to countries. Government departments in this period are under-resourced and have few established links with one another. It is very easy for different parts of government to pursue different agendas with competing priorities and goals, sometimes based on inconsistent data. Competing or conflicting initiatives can arise nationwide or in individual regions. Donors, also, too often pursue competing agendas based on priorities set in donor capitals rather than by beneficiary communities. At a time when joined-up government is particularly valuable, it is often particularly absent. Computers and data communications, linking government departments, donors, and other agencies can do a good deal to improve this situation, if urgent coordinated action is taken to build data-sharing networks early in the reconstruction process, though this still needs to be accompanied by political will and administrative competence. Developing and sharing common maps is one useful way of promoting information sharing. Coordination of government and donor agencies requires planning on the part of international agencies, including the selection of common standards and software to enable interoperability. It could also provide a starting point for later develop-ment of e-government.

In practice, all agencies and stakeholders involved in stabilization will make use of ICTs, particularly computers and communications devices, to pursue their objectives during the early period of reconstruction. That is simply part of how governments now work. The value of ICTs to reconstruction overall will be enhanced if their use of ICTs is coordinated, enabling information to be shared, and if it is establishes a platform for continuity with longer-term reconstruction and development. Coherence between ICT objectives and the deployment of physical infrastructure is also important and these can likewise be coordinated.

3.2 Infrastructure, Sector Policy, and Regulation

At the end of any significant violent conflict, national communications infra-structure is likely to be inadequate. Communications networks and equipment are often destroyed by combatants, either unintentionally or to deny communi-cations to their enemies. In any case, networks need to be regularly maintained, while technological change requires them to be frequently upgraded if they are to keep pace with those in other countries and with the services that users demand. The risks of investing in new or upgraded infrastructure in conflict-affected areas are too high for both governments and international businesses. Although there are exceptions—the introduction of mobile telephone networks by local entrepreneurs in Somalia being the most notable—countries are likely to emerge from violent conflict with less functioning communications infrastruc-ture than they had when violence began.

This presents a challenge and an opportunity. Good communications net-works are now considered essential for economic growth, and reinstating them forms part of the essential underpinning of economic recovery. Reestablishing communications can also help to rebuild national cohesion, restoring connections between urban and rural areas and family members. Early signs of tangible recov-ery, like connectivity, can build confidence that better times are on the way. For all these reasons it makes sense for governments and donors to prioritize com-munications infrastructure in reconstruction programmes. Four aspects of this have proved important.

- Firstly, the contribution which communications infrastructure makes to eco-nomic recovery depends on its **scope, quality, and capacity**. The last five years have seen increasing emphasis placed on broadband infrastructure, to the

The Role of Information and Communication Technologies in Postconflict Reconstruction
http://dx.doi.org/10.1596/978-1-4648-0074-0

extent that legacy networks, even where they survive, may now be thought inadequate. Where not already available, securing access to submarine cable networks—offering much higher bandwidth at much lower prices than satellites—must be a priority for governments and their international sponsors (as it was for Liberia and still is for Timor-Leste).[10] National backbone networks, extending the potential for broadband connectivity throughout the nation, are being increasingly prioritized by developing country governments and will require more investment where prior infrastructure has been destroyed or damaged. Early attention should be paid to the needs of economic sectors (which may also mean geographic regions) which are expected to drive economic recovery, but a planned approach to ensuring that effective connectivity reaches all populations nationwide can be important in reestablishing national cohesion. Universal access to communications is a desirable objective for postconflict governments.

- Secondly, **investment** needs to be secured to build this infrastructure. The shift to wireless technology has reduced the capital cost of network deployment (and security), but significant investment in physical infrastructure is required, particularly for international and national backbone connectivity. In practice, experience shows that the returns on new ICT investment in countries with poor communications are sufficient to attract mobile communications businesses to invest in postconflict countries very quickly, almost as the ink dries on their peace agreements.[11] Policy and regulatory decisions may be required in order to enable investors to invest, and should be prioritized. Funding may also be required from international donors, either in conjunction with private investment—subsidizing participation in a public-private partnership, as the World Bank has done in supporting Liberia's connection to the west African ACE cable—or to finance the extension of networks into more remote, less profitable, or more hazardous districts.

- Thirdly, the value of communications networks is partly dependent on wider national and regional infrastructure. Maximizing that value, including its contribution to reconstruction and social cohesion, depends significantly on **complementary infrastructures**, particularly those for power and transport. Reliable power supplies—or innovative alternatives—are required to run both operational and terminal equipment. Reliable and secure roads are needed to move equipment up-country and to facilitate the rebuilding of social and economic links stimulated by restored telecommunications. Private investors have proved more reluctant to finance these complementary infrastructures in the early years of peace, and more reliance on donor contributions is likely to be necessary.[12] The linkages and interactions between communications and other infrastructures require careful planning and donor coordination.

- Fourthly, experience shows that the **policy and regulatory environment** for communications plays a central role in establishing the scope, pace, and quality of the communications that become available. Open policy and regulatory approaches, which enable innovation, encourage investment in new technology and networks. Competitive markets, regulated to ensure interconnection and prevent abuse of market power, tend to expedite investment in fast-changing communications technologies and lower prices to end-users. Competitive, private sector markets are now the global norm, but those in countries emerging from long periods of violent conflict are often much less open, with higher levels of government involvement, constraints on private sector market entry, and participation and monopolistic or underdeveloped competitive markets. The World Bank has many years' experience in advising governments on the privatization, liberalization, and regulation of communications markets, and approaches to this in Rwanda and Timor-Leste are briefly described in case studies in this report. Early agreement on the process for communications restructuring—though this may itself be staged or gradual—should encourage investment and hasten the sector's contribution to reconstruction, the more so if it recognizes the importance of integrating and providing opportunities throughout the nation.

Infrastructure, sector policy, and regulation provide the necessary platform for the growth of ICT use in society and for ICT-enabled initiatives in reconciliation, public engagement, and development which are discussed below.

3.3 Reconciliation

One aspect of stabilization which has received increased attention recently is reconciliation, the building or rebuilding of trust between communities that have been in violent conflict, encouraging them to make use of governance institutions, elections and the media to resolve differences between them. Reconciliation is a complex process, requiring individuals and social groups to forgive, forget, and/or abandon long-standing discriminations, animosities, and, often, incidents that they regarded as atrocities. For it to work, the large majority of people need to recognize that the advantages which can be derived from reconciliation—in terms of security, opportunity, and quality of life—exceed the satisfactions of recrimination and, for some parties, the benefits of dominance. That requires both that the advantages of reconciliation are real and substantial, and that they are underpinned by enhanced communications that cut across the social, political, ethnic, religious, or other boundaries that divided people.

Many countries emerging from conflict have implemented some kind of formal Truth and Reconciliation Commission (TRC), often modelled on that which followed the end of apartheid in South Africa. TRCs provide an opportunity for those involved on both/all sides of a conflict, perpetrators and victims (and those who might be considered both), to record their experiences with the aim of developing shared understanding of what went wrong but might go right in future. They are not usually intended as part of judicial processes, but can work alongside them. They are more likely to be helpful where conflicts ended in stalemates or negotiated settlements rather than the outright victory of one or other party.

Surprisingly, perhaps, ICTs have not played a very prominent part in TRCs to date. Commissions have generally taken evidence in person rather than online, and even digital dissemination of evidence has been relatively limited. Experience in Liberia, reported in this volume, suggests that in that country, where Internet access is constrained, online dissemination of outcomes, which was in practice mainly accessed by the diaspora, was more significant than online evidence gathering. More could probably be done with this in other contexts, though the material gathered by TRCs is highly sensitive: constant reminders of hostility and atrocity can hinder as well as foster reconciliation, a point discussed further in section 3.4) below. Liberia's experience also draws attention to another important point—that, for many people, it is more important to address today's challenges of social cohesion and development rather than yesterday's failures.[13] Indeed, the perception that new media may be better used to address the future than the past may itself be a positive sign of reconciliation.

3.4 Media and Public Engagement

One of the most important discussions in recent thinking about postconflict reconstruction concerns the balance between stabilization and public participation in the rejuvenated polity. Some commentators, particularly donors and International Financial Institutions such as the World Bank, have seen rapid movement toward democracy and market competition—the characteristic features of liberal capitalist societies—as essential for establishing public confidence in a postconflict settlement and facilitating the economic growth that will reduce the risk of a return to violence. Others have argued that rapid democratization and market liberalization can be counterproductive in societies which lack stability: that individuals and groups that recently contested for power with armaments can exploit them either to undermine the new settlement or entrench their power within it. Social media can also be used to raise tensions between ex-combatants and communities emerging from conflict.[14] There is no disagreement here about the desirability of society moving toward greater inclusiveness in economic and political participation, but significant disagreement about the pace, sequencing, and appropriate constraints of liberalization.

ICTs, old and new, are at the heart of public debate and public participation. They provide the platforms and channels through which governments and politicians communicate to the population, and through which citizens feed back their concerns and views to those with power. Until relatively recently these platforms were dominated from above, by governments, politicians, and the owners of newspapers, radio, and television channels. The rapid spread of mobile phones through all sectors of the population in most countries, the emergence of the Internet, and particularly the arrival of services such as social networks, which are accessible by mobile phone as well as by personal computer (PC), have significantly altered the balance between those who control and those who use information and opinion platforms, by making it much easier for people to express and share their views in public. The emergence of these new platforms has made it harder to manage the relationship between stabilization and liberalization, as well as opening up new opportunities for public engagement.

Enthusiasm for new ICTs should not, here, obscure the importance of more traditional media. Television and, in many cases especially, radio are crucial sources of information for people who are living in or have recently suffered from violent conflict. Local radio can be a vital resource for people making judgements about their and their families' immediate security, or economic risks such as what and when to plant. Balanced and well-informed reporting can build confidence and support stabilization; broadcasts that are partisan or based on rumor can promote disharmony and spread anxiety.

The quality of broadcast media in postconflict situations is therefore of considerable significance to stabilization and reconciliation, as has been increasingly recognized by governments and donors in the last decade or so. Donor support has been significant because conventional sources of revenue for broadcasters, especially advertising, are in short supply in postconflict countries, particularly small low-income countries. Revitalizing traditional media is therefore often aid dependent.

While all donors have been keen to foster media plurality—in both ownership and political perspective—there have been differences of view, particularly where state-owned media are concerned. Some donors have preferred to foster an entirely private sector media environment, fearing that a state broadcaster would be little more than a partisan voice for government. Others have seen value in the European public service broadcasting model of a state-funded, but editorially independent and authoritative, news service.[15] Where revenue is short and journalistic standards are low, there are risks that media voices will spread rumor or entrench cultural differences in ways that threaten stabilization and the rebuilding of national identity. The experience of Radio Mille Collines, which fostered genocide in Rwanda in 1994, is a constant reminder to donors of the risks associated with partisan radio stations in postconflict countries (as Rwanda was considered up to the genocide).[16] "Warlord" radio stations can be found in Afghanistan and some other postconflict countries today.

Two approaches have been adopted by governments and donors to address these problems:

- The first, which has been led by donors, concerns the development of **media standards**. This involves training of journalists, the inculcation of journalistic ethics, the development of journalists' associations to support professionalism and editorial independence, and the establishment of news agencies with the competence and resources to research, validate, and share stories with diverse media outlets. Initiatives such as these require funding and expertise. In smaller, poorer countries, where advertising revenues are scarce, donor funding which has been used to finance broadcast start-ups may need to be continued much longer than has been normal practice if private media environments are not to become dominated by wealthy politicians.
- The second approach, which is more contentious and tends to be led by governments, concerns **media freedom**. Postconflict societies are generally volatile and vulnerable to the recrudescence of violence. Many people have not experienced media freedom for many years, if at all. Radio Mille Collines is

The Role of Information and Communication Technologies in Postconflict Reconstruction
http://dx.doi.org/10.1596/978-1-4648-0074-0

not the only example of broadcasting in a postconflict environment which has sought to foster hatred or discrimination. The International Covenant on Civil and Political Rights concedes that freedom of expression may be constrained to protect individuals' other rights and for the protection of national security and public order. It also requires the prohibition of "propaganda for war" and "advocacy of national, racial or religious hatred that constitutes incitement to discrimination, hostility or violence."[17] Some commentators feel strongly that free media can only operate effectively within a stable political environment, and that constraints on the freedom of media outlets to promote hatred and division are needed while the approaches to stabilization discussed at section 3.1 above become effective.[18]

This challenge of traditional media stems from the fact that broadcasting is not inherently inclusive. It disseminates content noninteractively, from one source to many listeners/viewers, while the costs of broadcasting mean that large-scale outlets will have only wealthy and/or highly motivated owners (though there are also opportunities for local and community radio). In marked contrast to broadcasting are the new media enabled by mobile telephony and the Internet, particularly social networking services such as Facebook and Twitter, Web 2.0 platforms such as blogs, and image-, audio-, and video-sharing websites. These have had three major effects on the communications environment in most societies today, all of which are particularly significant in those emerging from violent conflict:

- They enable individuals to publish anything they wish, information or opinion, true or false, verified or rumor, at virtually no cost, anonymously or pseudonymously if they so prefer.
- They extend the sources available to traditional news media to include non-professional content, including from material from "citizen journalists," and the range of news media outlets to include online as well as broadcast and paper publications.
- They extend the ability of individuals and groups to organize and microcoordinate activity, in public or in private, which may be supportive, hostile, or irrelevant to reconstruction and peacebuilding.

Many commentators believe that new media and interactive networks are already having a significant impact on what happens during conflicts and in the fluidity of postconflict environments. Where mobile phones are available, even in intermittently ungoverned countries like Somalia, vulnerable people use them to protect themselves from risk. Mobile phones and social networking clearly played a part in organizing opposition, coordinating protest, and building solidarity during the political transitions in North Africa that are commonly described as the Arab Spring. Their impact on these uprisings has sometimes been exaggerated—insurrections have taken place throughout history, long before Facebook and Twitter were on the scene—but their potency was recognized by governments that sought during the uprisings to block social networks, the Internet, or telecommunications in general. Mobile phones, the Internet, and social networks have continued to facilitate political organization after transition, as illustrated in the case study from Tunisia in this report.

Politics in society has been significantly changed by these developments. Those who are politically active now have new ways of being so and of coordinating with like-minded fellows. This has certainly extended participation in politics, reaching more people and enabling them to address more issues in more ways. New participatory models, such as Ushahidi, have taken advantage of networks of mobile and Internet users, using crowdsourcing to monitor rapidly changing events from natural disasters to political violence and the integrity of elections.[19] While they extend participation, however, these innovations do not necessarily increase its representativeness. More intensive users of communications, who are likely to be more active in political networks, are also likely to fall into particular social, income, age, and educational categories.

It is clear from experience in many countries that mass market mobile telephony, Internet, and social networking represent a change in the relationship between government, citizens, and media. The new, wide-reaching interactive connectivity which they provide enables people to engage more actively and effectively in public debate than previously, if they choose to do so. As with traditional media, empowered citizens can use new media in ways that support integration, stabilization, and reconstruction, or in ways that undermine them. New media are morally neutral. They can foster rumor and intercommunal hostility just as easily as they can facilitate democratic engagement and empower the marginalized. They have shifted power over this from a narrow range of media owners and managers to a much wider range of ICT end-users.

Most importantly, however, they are part of the new communications landscape for countries which emerge from violent conflict today. These shifts in the nature of media are not preventable this side of tyranny. Society will not revert from them, and their implications must be absorbed in plans for stabilization and public engagement. The challenge for governments and donors engaged in postconflict reconstruction is twofold:

- To maximize the value which old and new media can contribute, through public engagement, to political, social, and economic development
- To minimize the risk that they will be used to undermine stability and reconciliation.

Governments and donors are showing interest in responding to the former of these challenges. One critical issue for societies emerging from violent conflict is the establishment of alternative structures for the management of differences between recently hostile/combatant groups, structures which allow disputes to be addressed or resolved and policies to be developed peacefully.

Progress toward democracy is generally regarded as a central objective in meeting this challenge, and there is increasing awareness of the complexity of democratization in the transition from violent conflict. Elections—essentially the conduct and (it is hoped) resolution of conflict through votes rather than through violence—do not necessarily succeed in achieving this transition, particularly where political parties and electoral alliances replicate former combatant groups and where losers can easily return to arms.[20] ICTs have proved useful in monitoring, and thereby mitigating, party conduct, electoral violence, and fraud.

Successful democracy, however, consists of more than just elections. It requires checks and balances that protect the interests of minorities as well as enabling majority decision making, that ensure that the views of the poor and marginalized are considered alongside those of the wealthy and powerful, and that subject the actions of government to transparency and accountability. It is here, in particular, that the potential of new ICTs for enhancing participation and empowerment principally lies—valuable in all countries, and in all development processes, but perhaps particularly valuable in countries with entrenched suspicions and anxieties about future security. A good deal has been written about this, and the following paragraphs concentrate on just two aspects of it, consultation/public participation and open data.

3.4.1 Consultation

The fact that people are widely connected through new media makes it much easier for governments that wish to do so to assess public opinion, identify public concerns, and address public anxieties. The importance of early warning systems, identifying risks of recrudescent violence, was emphasized in section 3.1 above. These can now make use of crowdsourcing techniques, building on information from those at risk rather than relying on the top-down perceptions of officials, soldiers, and international observers. The example they provide can be more widely used to engage citizens in the reconstruction of the state. Crowdsourcing and other bottom-up approaches can be developed, for example to facilitate reporting of the abuse of power or corruption by officials, deficiencies in public services, perceptions of crime and personal security, and other indicators of progress (or otherwise) toward stabilization and development. These can be directed both at the general public and at selected groups of trusted informants.

Transparency and accountability, however, should be concerned with people's desires as well as with their fears. Evidence from the Liberian TRC experience shows that people are often more concerned to look for positive ways forward, contributing their thoughts about developmental needs. The opportunity exists now, through ICTs, to make public participation part of the culture of governance, including transparency and accountability, rather than a supporting mechanism for stabilization. There are many different ways in which public opinion can be solicited and gathered—from the traveling kiosks used by Liberia's TRC to radio phone-in programmes,[21] from opinion surveys conducted using mobile phones to crowdsourcing initiatives which encourage citizens to use their phones and other means to report on what is happening in their communities.

The cumulative evidence derived from these participatory sources is not, and should not be, solicited only by government, but by multiple stakeholders, including independent media and civil society. Such diversity is necessary because citizens will have different levels of confidence in different agencies, and also helps to develop a culture of open, trusted participation. While enhancing the information available to policy makers and their accountability to citizens, however, open participation does not necessarily overcome problems of ensuring that participation is representative. Some social groups (women in some societies, for example; religious minorities in others) are less likely or more fearful to participate. There is already evidence of deliberate manipulation of crowdsourcing to secure particular outcomes. Care needs to be taken to ensure that transparency and accountability extend to all sections of the community, particularly those that have been marginalized by conflict or feel vulnerable during reconstruction.

3.4.2 Open Data

Another aspect of transparency and accountability enhanced by ICTs—in all countries, not just those emerging from violent conflict—is open data. Governments today can obtain and analyse far more information about national circumstances than they could before modern data collection methods (including data derived from satellites) and before computerization. Information collected by governments can be made available much more widely than in the past, through traditional and new media. Instead of being restricted to narrow groups of officials, data access and analysis can be thrown open to the wider community, increasing transparency and accountability and enabling a wider range of (more or less) informed contributions to decision making. Business and civil society stakeholders, as well as governments and donors, can combine data from different sources to develop more sophisticated understandings of social trends, which can in turn facilitate policy making for stabilization and development. Although still in their infancy in developing countries, the World Bank has encouraged open data legislation and initiatives in countries including Kenya, where they have helped to build understanding of the developmental needs and quality of governance in different regions, an important factor in understanding the potential for violent conflict of the kind that affected the country following elections in 2007.[22]

In the long run, a culture of participatory governance, enabled and stimulated by ICTs, should help to build confidence in the institutions of the state, make government more responsive to citizens' needs, and ensure that differences between individuals and social groups are resolved peacefully rather than violently. There are, however, also risks that the openness of new media will be exploited by those who are hostile to reconstruction, as traditional media were exploited in Rwanda before the 1994 genocide. Policies that encourage public engagement need to recognize these risks and seek to mitigate them in the particular circumstances of individual countries. If they do so, then the more participatory environment enabled by ICTs should contribute positively toward long-term goals of economic and social development which represent the strongest bulwark against the return of violent conflict.[23]

3.5 Development

As noted earlier, countries with low levels of development (low *per capita* gross domestic product [GDP], poor income distribution, and dependence on primary commodity exports) are more prone to violent conflict. High rates of GDP growth, economic diversification, and inclusive distribution of social and economic gains are, therefore, generally thought likely to increase the stability of societies and reduce the risks of violence. There is, of course, no guarantee of this. Relatively prosperous societies can fall victim to civil war, especially if they are communally divided or prone to outside intervention—as did Lebanon, for example, in the 1970s/80s and Yugoslavia in the 1990s. Some societies with relatively high levels of GDP are highly dependent on the extraction of raw materials such as oil or diamonds, and have very poor income distribution, making them more vulnerable.

Nevertheless, it is generally agreed that achieving higher levels of economic and social development, with or without public participation, reduces the risk of differences descending into violence, and development is therefore a principal long-term goal of reconstruction. Experience suggests that the initial stages of recovery may see quite high rates of growth in economic indicators, from the very low levels experienced during conflict, but that the most crucial stages, building for the future, may be those that follow three to five years after peace agreements. As indicated in section 3.2 above, communications infrastructure is likely to be among the earliest sectors to attract investment. Experience also suggests that donor contributions tend to be concentrated in the early years and tail off during later periods of reconstruction when absorption capacity has increased and they might have more substantial impacts.[24]

Much more has been written about ICTs for development than about ICTs in postconflict reconstruction. The restructuring of telecommunications and spread of computing in the 1990s, followed by the rapid development of the Internet and mass markets for mobile telephony in developing countries, raised the profile of ICTs in development thinking. The World Summit on the Information Society (WSIS), held in two phases in Geneva, 2003, and Tunis, 2005, did much to stimulate the mainstreaming of ICTs in development planning and poverty reduction.[25] (It also gave birth to the ICT for Peace Foundation, based in Geneva.[26]) Many developing countries have adopted national ICT strategies, although these have not always been kept up to date. Countries that lack modern—which increasingly means broadband—communications infrastructures are considered likely to fall behind in competition for investment and therefore in development.[27] The importance of the role of ICTs in development is now, therefore, clearly established.

The contribution which ICTs can make to stabilization has been discussed above. This, together with subsequent paragraphs concerning infrastructure, reconciliation, and public engagement, provide a platform for the longer-term contribution of ICTs to development, economic growth and social welfare, and thereby to sustained recovery. This contribution is less specific to societies in postconflict reconstruction and more consistent with the experience of other developing countries than earlier dimensions of reconstruction considered in this chapter.

Before looking at particular initiatives of governments and donors, it should be recognized that ICTs are having profound impacts on society in general, as they are adopted and absorbed by citizens and businesses, irrespective of government intervention. These impacts extend to all aspects of society and economy, politics, and culture. While mobile telephony is the most visible ICT in popular use, increasing numbers of people, even in low-income countries, are gaining experience with computers at work or in education and are accessing the Internet through smartphones and cybercafés. Some are becoming adept, forming a nucleus of potential innovators in the use of online services and applications. Increasingly, these "tech-savvy" individuals are engaged in virtual networks which have the potential to lead opinion, coordinate protest or develop new applications as well as extending their range of social contacts.

The impact of these technologies on social behavior, interactions, and association, potentially subverting repressive governments or social norms, is well illustrated in the case study of Tunisia summarized in this report. Interventions by governments and donors play out on a rapidly changing underlying landscape of information and communications technology, services, and usage. Interventions and development programmes interact with that changing landscape, often unpredictably. Today's cutting-edge innovation is tomorrow's outmoded application. The developmental outcomes of ICTs are, in short, not in the hands of governments and donors, but of the citizens, professionals, businesses, and organizations that make use of them. Governments and donors can programme activities that aim to achieve desired objectives, particularly by establishing an enabling environment for the adoption and application of ICTs, but cannot guarantee the outcomes.

Many developing country governments have initiated national ICT strategies, and these can provide a framework for integrating ICTs into mainstream development objectives concerned with economic growth, poverty reduction, and social welfare. Rwanda's experience, described in this report, of four successive National Information and Communication Infrastructure Plans (NICIs), tied to the country's overall developmental *Vision* statement, is considered one of the most sophisticated ICT strategy processes in any developing or postconflict country. Strongly backed by President Kagame, who is a cochair of the UN Broadband Commission,[28] these NICIs have sought to build an ICT-enabled, knowledge-based economy through successive attention to sector restructuring, infrastructure and access, applications, and skill development.

Rwanda's experience illustrates the potential for ICT-enabled policy and the value of a well-defined strategic approach in directing and sequencing policies and programmes. It also illustrates some of the challenges that are likely to be experienced in low-income postconflict countries. While Rwanda's NICIs have achieved some of their goals, others have proved more elusive because of limited resources for investment, weaknesses in government capacity which restrict the country's ability to manage multiple streams of new activity, shortages in ICT and business skills in the community, and low awareness of the potential of ICTs to improve economic opportunity and social welfare. ICTs can help to address developmental challenges, but they cannot fix them alone, and are themselves often constrained by developmental weaknesses.

Many African countries have ICT strategies built around the NICI model which was originally developed by the UN Economic Commission for Africa.[29] Analysis of NICIs suggests that they focus on one or more of five broad objectives:

1. The use of ICTs to stimulate macroeconomic growth and integration into global economic structures
2. The development of ICT-specific sectors such as business process outsourcing and IT-enabled services
3. The use of ICTs to improve the range and quality of service delivery (in areas such as health and education)
4. Their use to improve the performance and coordination of government administration
5. The engagement of citizens in governance and decision making that concerns their lives.[30]

All but one of these—the second—are potentially applicable in all developing and postconflict countries. The fourth and fifth have already been discussed (at sections 3.1 and 3.4 above). The remaining paragraphs of this chapter briefly comment on those potential economic and social welfare impacts of ICTs on postconflict societies that are summarized in points 1 to 3.

As indicated above, economic success is, other things being equal, likely to reduce the risk of violence returning to postconflict states. Increased prosperity and reductions in poverty—not necessarily but preferably associated—will bind people into national reconstruction and raise the cost to them should peacebuilding fail, strengthening incentives to resolve conflict peacefully. (Growth which is dependent on oil or other primary commodities, like that in Timor-Leste, is less stabilizing.) The experience from ICT4D shows that ICTs contribute positively to economic growth in the following ways, which can be fostered by government and donors and included in strategic development plans.

- Firstly, the **communications environment** plays a significant part in attracting or deterring investment beyond the communications sector, and in facilitating or inhibiting trade. From an investment or business perspective, a communications environment will be attractive if it provides high-quality, reliable connectivity into receptive and substantial markets. Countries emerging from violent conflict usually have weak communications infrastructure and enabling regulatory environments, putting them at a disadvantage compared with neighbor countries. Rapid attention to these infrastructure and regulatory deficits, as in section 3.2 above, together with reduced business risk, should help to overcome this disadvantage and attract investment. ICTs can also be used to reduce the high costs which importers and exporters have experienced along trade routes. The sharing of data through public-private partnerships and "single window" approaches can eliminate costly delays, making hitherto unprofitable trade partnerships more viable.[31]

- Secondly, an expanding ICT sector can be a significant source of **employment**, an important factor in stabilizing societies with high levels of unemployment, particularly among ex-combatants. This stimulus to employment derives partly from opportunities for small-scale intermediary activity in the ICT sector itself, for example through airtime resale and mobile payments agents, maintenance, charging and resale of mobile phones, and local cybercafés; as well as the physical roll-out of infrastructure networks and, for more skilled personnel, the marketing and management of mobile phone and other businesses. The employment impact of mobile telephony, including that on women, is described in the Afghanistan case study in this report.

- The potential impact of ICTs on employment and entrepreneurship, however, spreads much further than the ICT sector alone. Much has been written about the ways in which **small-scale and micro-businesses** make use of mobile telephones to enhance their business opportunities. Particular attention has been paid to ways in which farmers and other small-scale producers use mobile phone access to price information databases to maximize returns on the sale of produce.[32] In practice, mobile phones are valuable throughout the supply chain, enabling farmers and other producers to purchase cheaper inputs and consumers to reduce their purchase costs, as well as potentially evening out supply and demand in fluctuating or seasonal markets. The range and sophistication of ICT use by developing country SMEs is growing as ICT devices become more pervasive. Social networks, for example, are beginning to be used as marketing platforms by small businesses.

- One application which has been recognized to have great potential is **mobile money**. Banking and capital markets are underdeveloped, especially in rural areas, in most developing countries and particularly underdeveloped in postconflict countries where financial services have been high-risk businesses. The success of the M-PESA mobile transaction service in Kenya, which enables money transfers using USSD (unstructured supplementary service data) and SIM ToolKit, both services available on all basic GSM mobile phones, has been widely discussed as a potential model for countries where banking services are rare. This is especially valuable in rural areas, where small businesses find it difficult to raise and maintain capital, and remittance transfers can be costly. Money transfer over mobile phones is potentially particularly attractive in postconflict situations where security is poor, people are anxious about the risks of travel, and remittances—from within the country or from

the diaspora—can be very important to both subsistence and economic recovery. Kenya's success with mobile money has not, however, been replicated
elsewhere with the same level of success, and more research is needed to understand the ways in which people in vulnerable communities develop confidence concerning financial transfers.[33]

- A further area in which economic interventions play a role—the second
  theme identified within NICI plans above—concerns support for the development of a more sophisticated **ICT or ICT-enabled sector**. Some governments—again including Kenya's—have invested hope and money in the
  development of a business process outsourcing (BPO) or IT-enabled service
  (ITES) sector, seeking to serve global markets in the manner pioneered in the
  Philippines and India. In practice, BPO/ITES sectors require a number of
  complementary factors to be viable—including high-quality, low-cost connectivity and a good supply of educated workers with relevant language skills
  in a relatively low-cost labor market. Some governments and international
  agencies have sought to stimulate ICT and ICT-enabled business activity
  through incubators and other incentives to investment.[34] Larger developing
  countries, such as Kenya and South Africa, are seeing the emergence of entrepreneurial ICT sectors concerned with software and application development, web design and so on.[35] The emergence of such sectors, localizing more
  ICT activity and reducing dependence on imported expertise, could have a
  catalytic impact on local economies, where they are enabled by market size
  and facilitated by education and training.

Quantifying the cumulative value of these outcomes is far from easy, though
efforts have been made to do so.[36] From the perspective of postconflict reconstruction, it is probably most important that they are understood in relation to
national circumstances. Only some countries, for example, have the right combination of communications, business and human skills to offer BPO or ITES services in international markets, or to use ICTs to stimulate tourism (another common aspiration). Not many countries can fulfil the ambition expressed in many
national ICT strategies, to become a communications hub within their region.
Small countries with limited educational facilities are unlikely to become centers
of ICT innovation but can benefit from small-scale training and maintenance in
ICTs. Some postconflict countries have much greater potential than others to
build dynamic new sectors, such as tourism, which can take advantage of both
technology and peace. Public-private partnerships—involving international agencies, governments, and the private sector—could be particularly valuable in leveraging investment where the level of risk continues to be considered high.

Much the same points as have been made about economic prosperity and
poverty reduction can be made about ICTs in service delivery and social welfare.
Governments and donors have been keen to build on the potential of ICTs to
enhance the provision and quality of public services such as health and education. NGOs have also gained considerable experience in using ICTs for social
welfare, from computer databases managing hospital supplies to reminding

patients by SMS to take their medicines, from supporting teacher training to distance education and open educational resources. There is no space here to explore these applications in depth, but their implications for postconflict reconstruction can be illustrated from these two sectors:

Conflict is harmful to **health**. It disrupts hospitals and the supply of medicines. Doctors and clinicians leave the country to work elsewhere. Conflict injuries, rape, and mutilation add to the catalogue of challenges faced by depleted medical staff, as traumatized victims, mostly civilians, seek help. There is high risk of epidemics, from cholera to human immunodeficiency virus (HIV), spreading extensively as displaced and vulnerable populations migrate within and beyond national borders. These impacts of war on health have lasting legacies. Postconflict societies have more people who are psychologically traumatized, physically disabled, weakened by malnutrition or suffering from chronic illnesses.

There are many different ways in which ICTs have contributed to improving health outcomes in developing countries, which typically experience high levels of poor health, high risk of epidemic, and low levels of clinical expertise of the kind also found in postconflict countries. ICTs play an increasingly important part in monitoring health and providing early warning of epidemics; in administering hospitals and health services and managing drug supplies; in providing diagnostic and other support to clinicians working in remote or hazardous areas; in promoting healthier lifestyles, behaviors, and practices; in coordinating vaccinations and providing patients and the public with health advice. While some of this is new activity enabled by ICTs, much of it depends on the exploitation of ICTs' potential for better information management and analysis and for improving the organization of bureaucracies. Gains can be made both in the immediate aftermath of violent conflict, as clinicians struggle with the consequences of ill-health, and in the longer term as healthier populations become more economically productive.

Education is the other area of social and economic development in which ICTs have been most extensively deployed, and in which they may help to address specific challenges in postconflict contexts. Education, like health services, breaks down in civil war. After prolonged conflict, a generation may have been educated in violence rather than in school. Addressing that generation's educational deficits, giving individuals more opportunities to develop skills, gain and exploit capabilities, and earn livelihoods through productive work, plays an important part in increasing incentives for peace within society.

Nor can adults be neglected. Training ex-combatants and others who have lost out on schooling, enabling them to secure employment or start businesses rather than relying on the skills they learnt in uniform, is important for both social inclusion and economic opportunity.

ICTs and distance learning, including mobile applications, can play a part in overcoming shortfalls in teaching staff, facilities, and resources. ICT skills themselves are likely to be in very short supply in postconflict countries, and can be a particular focus for interventions, including support for independent, private sector training. As time proceeds, as in all developing countries, governments and donors can focus on wider applications of ICTs in education, from management information systems to open educational resources, teacher training, and the supply of low-cost forms of access.[37]

Notes

1. Collier et al. (2003), "Breaking the Conflict Trap.".

2. The relationship between ICTs and conflict prevention is explored, with case studies, in Francesco Mancini, ed. (2013), "New Technology and the Prevention of Violence and Conflict," UNDP/USAID/IPI.

3. See, for example, Michael L. Best et al. (n.d.), "Uses of Mobile Phones in Post-Conflict Liberia," Georgia Institute of Technology, available at http://mikeb.inta.gatech.edu/uploads/papers/qsort.Liberia.pdf.

4. The complex broadcasting environment in Afghanistan is explored in BBC Media Action (2012), "The Media of Afghanistan: The Challenges of Transition," available at: http://downloads.bbc.co.uk/mediaaction/policybriefing/bbc_media_action_afghanistan_is_in_transition.pdf.

5. See, *for example*, Search for Common Ground (n.d.), "Communication for Peacebuilding: Practices, Trends and Challenges," available at http://www.sfcg.org/resources/Communications_for_Peacebuilding_Report_2June2011.pdf.

6. http://www.realtechsupport.org/UB/MRIII/papers/CollectiveIntelligence/Ushahidi.pdf.

7. Gabriel Gatehouse for BBC News, (20132, March 8), "Kenya Election: 'Tech Hub' Hopes Take Polling Day Blow," at http://www.bbc.co.uk/news/world-africa-21712715.

8. See www.uchaguzi.co.ke.

9. Helena Puig Larrauri, (2013), "New Technologies and Conflict Prevention in Sudan and South Sudan."

10. See case study chapters.

11. John Bray (2005), "International Companies and Post-Conflict Reconstruction: Cross-sectoral Comparisons," World Bank, available at http://www-wds.worldbank.org/external/default/WDSContentServer/WDSP/IB/2005/03/30/000012009_20050330161732/Rendered/PDF/31819.pdf.

12. ibid.

13. Thomas N. Smyth et al., (n.d.), "MOSES: Exploring New Ground in Media and Post-conflict Reconciliation," Georgia Institute of Technology, available at http://mikeb.inta.gatech.edu/uploads/papers/pap0922-smyth.pdf.

14. See for example Anna Matveeva (2013), "Conflict Cure or Curse? Information and Communication Technologies in Kyrgyzstan."

15. See BBC Media Action (2012); also Sheldon Himelfarb (2010), "Media and Peacebuilding in Afghanistan," United States Institute of Peace, available at http://www.usip.org/files/resources/PB15%20Media%20and%20Peacebuilding%20in%20Afghanistan.pdf.

16. Tim Allen and Nicole Stremlau (2005), "Media Policy, Peace and State Reconstruction," London School of Economics Crisis States Research Centre, available at http://www.crisisstates.com/Publications/dp/dp08.htm.

17. http://www.ohchr.org/EN/ProfessionalInterest/Pages/CCPR.aspx.

18. for example, Roland Paris (2004), *At War's End: Building Peace After Civil Conflict*, Cambridge University Press.

19. For a discussion of crowdsourcing in this context, see Maja Bott and Young Gregor (2011), "'The Role of Crowdsourcing for Better Governance in International Development," World Bank, available at http://www.scribd.com/doc/75642401/The-Role-of-Crowdsourcing-for-Better-Governance-in-Fragile-State-Contexts.

20. See, for example, Paris (2004).

21. See Smyth, Etherton, and Best (2010).

22. Kenya's open data website is at https://opendata.go.ke/.

23. See Cesar Brod (2013).

24. Collier et al. (2003), "Breaking the Conflict Trap."

25. The World Summit's outcome documents are at www.itu.int/wsis.

26. See www.ict4peace.org.

27. See for example, the perceptions of the Broadband Commission for Digital Development, made up of international organizations, senior ICT sector personnel, and other opinion leaders, at http://www.broadbandcommission.org/.

28. See www.broadbandcommission.org.

29. http://www.uneca.org/sites/default/files/publications/nici-book.pdf.

30. Unpublished work by David Souter and Abiodun Jagun for UNDP.

31. Lishan Adam, David Souter et al., "Transformation-Ready: The strategic application of information and communication technologies in Africa: Regional Trade and Integration Sector Study," African Development Bank and World Bank (2012), available at http://siteresources.worldbank.org/EXTINFORMATIONANDCOMMUNICATIONANDTECHNOLOGIES/Resources/282822-1346223280837/RegionalTradeandIntegration_Fullreport.pdf.

32. See for example, Jenny C. Aker and Isaac M. Mbiti (2010), "Mobile Phones and Economic Development in Africa," *Journal of Economic Perspectives*, available at http://sites.tufts.edu/jennyaker/files/2010/09/aker_mobileafrica.pdf.

33. See Kevin Donovan (2012), "Mobile Money," in World Bank, *Information and Communication for Development 2012: Maximising Mobile*, available at http://siteresources.worldbank.org/EXTINFORMATIONANDCOMMUNICATIONANDTECHNOLOGIES/Resources/IC4D-2012-Report.pdf.

34. See for example, *info*Dev's incubator initiative at http://www.infodev.org/en/TopicBackground.8.html.

35. See UNCTAD, "Information Economy Report 2012: The Software Industry and Developing Countries," available at http://unctad.org/en/PublicationsLibrary/ier2012_en.pdf.

36. For example, International Telecommunication Union (2012), "Impact of Broadband on the Economy," available at http://www.itu.int/ITU-D/treg/broadband/ITU-BB-Reports_Impact-of-Broadband-on-the-Economy.pdf.

37. See Lishan Adam, Neil Butcher et al. (2012), "Transformation-Ready: The Strategic Application of Information and Communication Technologies in Africa: Education Sector Study," African Development Bank & World Bank, available at: http://siteresources.worldbank.org/EXTINFORMATIONANDCOMMUNICATIONANDTECHNOLOGIES/Resources/282822-1346223280837/Education_Fullreport.pdf

Summary and Recommendations

Part One of this report has presented an overview and examples of the relationship between information and communication technologies (ICTs) and postconflict reconstruction. What does the evidence available—in this chapter, in the case studies that accompany it and in the literature more generally—suggest should be priorities for governments and donors working in postconflict countries?

The first point, which should be emphasized again, is that **different countries pose different challenges and different opportunities**. Postconflict countries differ markedly from one another in size and level of economic development, in economic and social structures, in the causes of conflict, the ways in which conflicts have been ended, and the legacies they leave behind. Differences between middle-income countries and least developed countries (LDCs) are likely to be particularly pronounced. The ICT environments of postconflict countries will also differ markedly. There is no single prescription for ICT-enabled peacebuilding or for the role of ICTs in reconstruction which can be applied across the board. Successful approaches to ICTs in reconstruction will be rooted in a thorough understanding of national political, economic, social, cultural, and communications contexts.

Having said that, **postconflict societies nevertheless share certain common characteristics which are relevant to ICT-enabled intervention**. Social cohesion has been disrupted by violence, leaving legacies of hostility, suspicion, and insecurity which need to be overcome if countries are not to follow the experience of many and revert to violence. Economic production and trade will also have been disrupted, resulting in underemployment, underinvestment, and underperformance—a problem for today but a platform on which recovery can build. Substantial numbers of people are likely to have gone into exile, taking skills and capital with them, but also offering the potential that those skills and capital will return (as well as of investment and remittances). Infrastructure, including communications infrastructure, is likely to have been destroyed but can be restored.

The ICT sector will not be the first priority of governments and donors in postconflict reconstruction, though it is likely to be one of the first to bring tangible economic benefits. Stabilization requires the rebuilding of political institutions, the reintegration of former combatants, the establishment and maintenance of physical security, the restoration of critical economic sectors such as oil or mineral extraction, the injection of capital into the financial system, the production and distribution of food supplies, and the restoration of health and education services. The ICT sector is one among many competitors for the attention of policy makers and practitioners in this complex reconstruction context. The evidence suggests, however, that it has an increasingly important part to play in reconstruction, not just as a sector in itself but as a cross-cutting sector, built around a general purpose technology, which can contribute to reconstruction across the board. This impact can be felt from early stages in reconstruction, including stabilization. The sector can also help in generating income, from fees paid by investors, from taxation of communications usage, and, in the form of foreign exchange, from incoming calls made by relief agencies and those in the diaspora. It merits more attention than it has sometimes been paid.

Chapter 1 identified five broad themes of reconstruction:

- Stabilization
- Infrastructure
- Reconciliation
- Public engagement
- Development.

Chapter 3 reviewed the contribution which ICTs can make to each of these. How can that contribution as a whole be summarized?

- The first objective of reconstruction, many would now argue, is **stabilization**. Unless people feel secure, government institutions regain credibility, and the rule of law replaces the threat of violence, then societies will be vulnerable to the recurrence of violence and unable to secure the developmental gains that build social and economic cohesion (and *vice versa*). From the point of view of reconstruction, therefore, the most important question about ICTs in the early period following the end of violence concerns the contribution they can make to stabilization. Chapter 3 discussed a number of areas in which ICTs can make an important contribution, including the coordination of government and donor activity, from humanitarian relief to administration, and the establishment of effective early warning systems built on public participation.
- Much of the rest of the discussion above is concerned with ways in which governments and donors can use ICTs to build from short-term stabilization and recovery to **long-term stability and development**. There is a natural continuum between these as, it is hoped, over time peace becomes less fragile. Stabilization measures in postconflict reconstruction should look forward to and enable longer-term social and economic development. The reforms and interventions made through ICTs should likewise elide from stabilization to development.

4.1 Stabilization

The fact that mobile communications companies are generally keen to invest quickly in postconflict countries is a powerful starting point for governments and donors. Those companies are likely to start planning for investment before peace agreements are signed or political transitions come about, so that they can take advantage of first-mover status. Strategic planning for the ICT sector needs to be just as nimble if it is to maximize the advantage of this investment opportunity and avoid the risk of suboptimal market outcomes. Donors and other stakeholders should think ahead about transition, and potential ICT initiatives, before the urgency of reconstruction is upon them.

This does not necessarily mean that liberalization and privatization should be accelerated: the pace of restructuring needs to be considered in the context of overall political and economic stabilization as well as the long-term interests of the communications market. However, early action should be taken to facilitate investment, ensuring that it works to the benefit of the country concerned as well as that of investing companies, promotes rather than inhibits the development of competition (for example though open access regulation) and encourages inclusive network deployment and access nationwide (including marginalized and/or defeated population groups). Critical infrastructure gaps, such as international cable connectivity and reliable connectivity in major industrial and business centers, should be addressed as priorities to help achieve rapid economic gains.

In the medium term, as the immediate risks of the transition from violence to peace recede, the focus of reconstruction shifts from stabilization to the consolidation of stability and to longer-term development. This process may take a decade before reconstruction can be said to be complete. ICTs' contribution, over this time, also shifts from stabilization to the consolidation of peace and to development.

4.2 Consolidating Stabilization

Chapter 3 explored some of the ways in which ICTs can contribute to consolidating stabilization, by addressing the welfare challenges of postconflict countries, helping people to manage in insecure environments, and building confidence, between communities and in the long-term prospects that peace will be sustained. Three aspects of this can be emphasized.

- Postconflict societies suffer from specific **economic, social, and humanitarian challenges** which result from the experience that they have gone through. In cases of prolonged warfare, these include economic disruption, increased poverty and vulnerability; the loss of expertise through migration and the displacement of many people from their homes; increased vulnerability to disease and (likely) higher rates of HIV, malaria, and tubercular infections; a generation educated in violence rather than in school; underemployment exacerbated by large numbers of ex-combatants with the wrong kind of skills.

The Role of Information and Communication Technologies in Postconflict Reconstruction
http://dx.doi.org/10.1596/978-1-4648-0074-0

Other societies—for example, those that have seen power transferred through briefer insurrections—will have suffered less. ICTs form part of the range of instruments available to citizens, governments, and donors in addressing these challenges at the boundaries between humanitarian relief and development.

- **Reconciliation** is another necessary part of the consolidation of stability. Previously divided communities at least need to accommodate their different interests. ICTs can play a part in this informally by building channels of communication between communities, and in more formal processes such as Truth and Reconciliation Commissions.
- More widely, **public participation** in governance is increasingly seen as an essential component in building the social cohesion that is required for transition from violent conflict to democratic competition. This transition is complex. Those who are managing the process of transition need to disseminate accurate information and dispel rumor. Press and broadcasting freedom need to be introduced in ways that foster plurality of ownership and views, but discourage attempts to divide communities and revert to violence. The potential for state and public sector broadcasting needs to be considered carefully within this context.

New ICTs meanwhile are changing the landscape of communications, making it much easier for citizens to communicate, publish, and organize autonomously, without requiring the intermediation, as publishers, of traditional media. How people make use of new media is beyond the control of authority, a genuinely new development in society that occurs alongside any process of reconstruction and reconciliation. Governments and donors can take advantage of new ICTs to encourage public engagement in peaceful political development, for example by using crowdsourcing techniques to gather evidence and views, by providing more accessible consultation processes and by making official data open for public use. Care still needs to be taken to ensure that evidence gathered is representative of all sections of society.

4.3 Development

In the longer term, as the risk of a return to violence recedes, reconstruction merges into development, and the role of ICTs becomes increasingly similar to that in comparable developing countries that have not experienced violent conflict. Much has been written about the potential value of ICTs in enabling economic growth and poverty reduction, social welfare, health and education, and some examples of this are described in chapter 3. Strategic approaches to Information and communication technology for development (ICT4D) have become common, but their success is likely to be dependent on three factors: the extent to which they are rooted in a thorough understanding and realistic assessment of the country concerned; the extent to which they are integrated into more comprehensive development policies and programmes; and the extent to which they recognize the need for policies and practice to adjust continually in response to changing technology, market, and other circumstances. ICT4D strategies in postconflict countries need to recognize and address those countries' particular legacies, challenges, and risks, as well as the more general challenges and risks experienced by comparable developing countries (see Box 4.1). Where the latter are concerned, there will also be substantial differences between countries with different development characteristics, particularly between middle-income countries with diverse economies, on the one hand, and low-income countries dependent on raw material exports, on the other.

Box 4.1 Policy Recommendations

The analysis in this report, including its country chapters, and in other recent international studies, shows that ICTs can add substantial real value to postconflict reconstruction, from supporting stabilization in the immediate aftermath of violence to facilitating the long-term development that makes return to violence less likely. While the contribution which ICTs can make has some common characteristics across all contexts, associated with the five themes of postconflict reconstruction identified in the first chapter, it will vary in important ways from one context to another. Societies emerging from violent conflict are fragile, as is the process of reconstruction itself. ICT interventions of the kinds described in this report can help to accelerate social and economic reconstruction but, like all interventions in postconflict societies, must be carefully integrated with other reconstruction measures to maximize value and mitigate any risks associated with them.

Six recommendations emerge from the report for governments and international agencies—including security, humanitarian, and development agencies—concerned with postconflict reconstruction. These are as follows:

1. **ICT strategies for reconstruction need to be rooted in specific national contexts and integrated with other stabilization and reconstruction initiatives.** Research and analysis, involving all relevant stakeholders, are essential for the development of approaches which respond to the social, economic, and political challenges of individual postconflict states. As in other areas of postconflict reconstruction, it is important that interventions made by different agencies are consistent with one another in the way that they respond to national needs.

2. **Stabilization is the most important priority in the immediate aftermath of conflict.** Without security and stability, it will be impossible to rebuild infrastructure and establish lasting economic recovery. Security, humanitarian, and development agencies should plan ahead for the rapid deployment of emergency ICT networks that will facilitate stabilization, including early warning systems that will help to avoid the recrudescence of violent conflict.

3. **Communications networks should be a priority in rebuilding national infrastructure.** International communications businesses have shown that they are prepared to invest in mobile telecommunications networks very soon after the signature of peace agreements. The rapid reestablishment of communications networks will facilitate social cohesion and

box continues next page

The Role of Information and Communication Technologies in Postconflict Reconstruction
http://dx.doi.org/10.1596/978-1-4648-0074-0

Box 4.1 Policy Recommendations *(continued)*

economic recovery. Governments should take urgent action to remove legal and regulatory barriers to investment and issue competitive licences for communications operators. International agencies can provide essential expertise where this is concerned.

4. **Opportunities for citizen engagement in reconstruction should be fostered, but also monitored to ensure that they are inclusive and do not become vehicles for advocating renewed conflict.** New and online media offer new opportunities for public expression and for transparency and accountability which can be powerful agents for empowerment and inclusiveness. They can also contribute to formal "truth and reconciliation" processes. However, new and traditional media can also be abused by those hostile to reconstruction and reconciliation. Development actors should invest in media training and facilitate diverse ownership and inclusive participation in all forms of media.

5. **ICT strategies should form part of plans for long-term reconstruction and development.** It is now widely agreed that ICTs contribute substantially to social and economic development. There is wide-ranging experience from developing countries of their increasing value in health and education, agriculture, and enterprise development. National strategies which include infrastructure, access, and applications development, built on a careful understanding of local communications markets and priorities, increase the likelihood that ICTs will enable sustainable developmental gains. They should be included in national development planning from an early stage.

6. **Development agencies should share experience of ICTs in postconflict reconstruction more effectively.** There is a growing body of experience of the use of ICTs in postconflict contexts. While contexts vary, more extensive experience sharing would enable governments and development agencies to make more effective use of ICTs at all stages of postconflict work, from short-term stabilization to long-term development.

4.4 Conclusions

This overview suggests that those involved in reconstruction need to think carefully about the potential value of ICTs. They need to recognize, firstly, that ICTs, particularly mobile telephony, the Internet, and social networking, will have an impact on social and economic development which is independent of any government or donor activity. In some ways this may threaten efforts at reconstruction, in others reinforce them. Governments and donors should assess the threats and opportunities involved, seeking in their policies and programmes to minimize the former and maximize the latter. They will be more effective in doing so if they coordinate their activities with one another, seek input from target beneficiaries and engage communications businesses and developers in policy and programme design.

The discussion has emphasised the importance of sequencing interventions, beginning with stabilization, enabling the early reinstatement of communications infrastructure, leading toward the consolidation of gains made in the early period of reconstruction, reconciliation, and longer-term development. While approaches need to be adjusted as time proceeds, in line with circumstances, an overall strategic framework encompassing the whole period of reconstruction, including the liberalization of media and communications markets, would be valuable. It should be recognized from the start that reconstruction requires long-term commitment in terms of funding and political will.

No review of the experience of ICTs and conflict can end, however, on any note of certainty. As has been emphasized above, conflicts are very diverse, taking place in different countries and different contexts, with very different outcomes. The relationship between national conflict and international relations has changed and continues to change with the ebb and flow of global power. The last ten to fifteen years have seen considerable changes in the understanding of conflict, its relationship with development and the roles which governments, donors, and other international actors can and should be playing. As for ICTs, their technology and markets are in constant change, enabling new possibilities, and some new challenges, as new technologies become available and then more widely available in postconflict situations. The impact of ICTs on society in general is both growing and in constant flux; their impact on postconflict societies is not likely to be otherwise. This suggests a need for ongoing research that continually reinforms our understanding—ensuring that, as well as learning from experience today, we recognize that tomorrow's experience will differ from it.

4.5 Further Research

It is clear from the case studies in this programme of work, from current work on ICTs and conflict being undertaken by United Nations Development Programme (UNDP) and other agencies, academics, and civil society practitioners, that there is much about today's experience that we also need to understand better than we do. This chapter therefore concludes with two suggestions for further research.

Firstly, individual case studies of ICTs and conflict, such as those in this volume and others published in academic and practitioner literature, rarely look at the holistic impact of ICTs and communications on the societies with which they are concerned. The relationship between ICTs, society, and postconflict reconstruction is both complex and variable. While it is possible to draw useful conclusions from collages of national experience concerning different aspects of ICTs, less impressionistic, more holistic assessments of four or five postconflict countries would be extremely valuable. Comprehensive assessments of this kind would help to compare the interaction between ICTs and context more effectively, as well as grasping the interactions between different aspects of ICTs and different aspects of reconstruction. In addition to assessments which look back at recent experiences, much could be learnt from new studies initiated at the point of transition from violence to stabilization, whenever opportunities arise to do this. Studies of this kind could be continued through the reconstruction period,

The Role of Information and Communication Technologies in Postconflict Reconstruction
http://dx.doi.org/10.1596/978-1-4648-0074-0

up to a decade long, engaging peacekeeping as well as development expertise and interest in an ongoing process of research, analysis, and learning.

Secondly, there are a number of specific issues on which the evidence reviewed for this chapter suggests a need for greater understanding, including more research, where this would have real value for governments, international agencies, and other practitioners as they go about contributing to reconstruction. Four areas are suggested in particular for this more rigorous and systematic treatment:

1. The relationship between ICTs and stabilization, including infrastructure and application priorities
2. The ways in which communities emerging from violent conflict make use of ICTs in building their own social networks, particularly among returning migrants and between home communities and diasporas
3. The relationship between old and new media as vehicles for managing ongoing tensions, building social cohesion and facilitating reconciliation
4. The relationship between ICTs, employment generation, and entrepreneurship in postconflict environments.

Finally, the extent to which these and other aspects of ICTs and their potential are explored in the postconflict literature is disappointing. As in many other areas of the relationship between ICTs and public policy, there is a need for more dialogue between academic and practitioner experts in both fields. The World Bank, which has been active for many years in each, is well-placed to facilitate this.

PART II

CHAPTER 5

Introduction to the Case Studies

The following five chapters summarize case studies of the experience of information and communication technologies (ICTs) in countries which have emerged from conflict in the relatively recent past. These case studies—which are reported at greater length on the World Bank website—are not intended to give a comprehensive view of experience in the countries concerned, but to illustrate different aspects of the ways in which ICTs have interacted with and can enhance the potential for reconstruction and development. Insights from them have been incorporated in Part 1 of the report. In addition, this Part of the report draws on experience from two countries emerging from conflict—Somalia (see Box 5.1) and South Sudan (see Box 5.2)—where the World Bank Group has begun new engagements.

Three points should be understood by way of preface to these country studies.

Firstly, it should be remembered that these countries' experience with ICTs has taken place within a context of very rapid global change in information and communications technology and markets. Since the beginning of the twenty-first century, access to telephony, which was once the privilege of government, big business, and the rich, has become available to the large majority of people even in low-income countries. Mobile devices have replaced fixed phones as the primary communications interface for individuals, and have acquired many complementary functions. The Internet has become close to ubiquitous in industrial countries and increasingly widely available, especially now on mobile devices, in developing countries. Digital social networks, absent at the turn of the century, have become foundations of many people's personal and social identities, in industrial and increasingly in developing countries. Technical innovations such as cloud computing and new lifestyle and developmental applications are continually changing the scope of digital experience. These technological and market changes have in turn had major impacts on social behavior, economic organization, political engagement, and development potential. It is not easy to disentangle what is exceptional in individual countries' experience from this global phenomenon.

Secondly, as noted in Part 1 of the report, the experience of conflict varies substantially from one country to another. Each of the countries discussed in the following chapters has had a different experience.

- Afghanistan has seen two decades of civil war, followed by international intervention (in 2001), the installation of an elected government and ongoing reconstruction and development efforts in a context of continuing insurgency.
- Liberia also suffered two decades of chaotic civil war, in its case ended by negotiation in 2003, also followed by a decade of reconstruction and development but without continued violent conflict.
- Rwanda, with a long history of instability and insecurity, experienced genocide, invasion and civil war in 1994, resulting in the deaths of 10 percent of its population and exile of many more. It has avoided internal violent conflict since then, while its government has pursued a development strategy which emphasizes ICTs.
- In Timor-Leste, an independence referendum in 1999—itself an outcome of years of conflict between Indonesian authorities and Timorese rebels—led to destructive violence which was brought to a halt by international peacemaking. Independence was itself disrupted by violent internal conflict in 2006.
- Tunisia, by contrast with the other countries studied, has not experienced civil war but saw decades of authoritarian rule end in rapid insurrection during 2011, followed by a process of democratization which is ongoing.

The roots of these conflicts and their routes to resolution have varied significantly—the latter including international intervention, negotiation, and victory for one side in the conflict. Each country studied has achieved a different level of postconflict reconstruction and security, with governance and government institutions in some still highly fragile. Tunisia's experience of short-term insurrection differs most markedly from the other countries studied, as its period of conflict was much shorter and less violent. Tunisia is also more prosperous than the other countries studied, which are least developed countries (LDCs) dependent on agriculture and/or raw material extraction.

Thirdly, the case studies look at different aspects of the complex relationship between ICTs, reconstruction, and development.

- The case studies of Afghanistan and Timor-Leste report in general terms on the development of the ICT sector and on ways in which ICTs have contributed to social and economic change within those countries.
- The study of Rwanda also reviews the development of the ICT sector in general, focusing on its government's successive national plans for information and communications for development (ICT4D) and on four particular development programmes.
- The chapter on Liberia explores three separate aspects of ICTs in that country's recent experience—the policy process which led to Liberia accessing

international submarine fiber, the experience of cybercafé users in the capital Monrovia, and use of the Internet in the country's national reconciliation process.

- The chapter on Tunisia explores the relationship between communications and wider social and economic forces in the country before, during and since its recent insurrection.

Each of these different experiences and emphases contributes to the overall assessment of ICTs, reconstruction, and development which is included in Part 1 of the report.

Box 5.1 The Need to Communicate Transcends Both War and Peace: The Case of Somalia

Like most sectors of the Somali economy, the information and communication technologies (ICTs) sector is in a poor state following two decades of civil war and terrorist activity, a period during which there was effectively no functioning government. The fixed-line network of the pre-1990 state–owned incumbent telecommunications operator was effectively destroyed. As a result, rates of penetration of ICTs are now amongst the lowest in the world. Somalia was one of only four African countries (along with Central African Republic, Eritrea and South Sudan) that missed the December 2012 deadline, set by the African Union in 2007, to connect all African capitals with fiber-optic cable. In November 2013, the EASSY undersea cable arrived in Mogadishu and is due to be in service in early 2014. The Internet is used by only 3 percent of the population, at best, and the lack of secure and affordable communications is one of many barriers holding back the donor community in its efforts to bring aid and development to the country.

Nevertheless, there are important positive aspects to the ICT sector in the country, especially mobile communications. Despite—or perhaps because of—the lack of regulation, private, unlicensed mobile companies, using satellite for international communications, have emerged to serve high demand for communications, especially between Somalia and the large Somali diaspora. Between seven and ten mobile phone companies are present in the regions known as Somaliland, Puntland, or South and Central Somalia, and some are present in all three (see figure 5.1). Despite an absence of foreign commercial investment, companies like Hormuud Telecom now provide service to around two million subscribers in Somalia and have introduced 3G mobile services since the start of 2013. Despite having to change headquarters three times due to terrorist activity, Hormuud has managed to remain profitable and has continued to grow. Its EVC+ service, which facilitates exchange of airtime credit among users, has become a virtual currency within the country, given the lack of faith in the Somali shilling and the difficulty of using US dollars for low-value transactions. Somalia is also attracting start-up companies such as Somalia Wireless, which established itself as a leading Internet Service Provider within one year of its founder's return to the country. Somalia Wireless is now planning to invest in a "Super Wifi" network to serve its growing user base around Mogadishu.

box continues next page

The Role of Information and Communication Technologies in Postconflict Reconstruction
http://dx.doi.org/10.1596/978-1-4648-0074-0

Box 5.1 The Need to Communicate Transcends Both War and Peace: The Case of Somalia (continued)

Figure 5.1 Major Mobile Operators and Estimated Market Shares in Somalia, December 2012

Operator	Regions active	Networks (launch year)	Estimated market shares
Hormuud Telecom (Hortel)	South and Central Somalia only	GSM 900 (2005) GPRS (2007) 3G (W-CDMA) (2013)	*Note: Estimates of the size of the mobile market in Somalia vary widely, but is probably around 2 million mobile subscriptions at 31 Dec 2013 out of a population of around 10 million. Source: TeleGeography Inc.*
*Telecom Somalia	Major cities	GSM 900 (2001)	
Nationlink	Major cities	GSM 900 (2001)	
Telesom	Somaliland only	GSM 900/1800 (1999) 3G W-CDMA (2011)	
Somafone	Most regions	GSM 900/1800 (2005) GPRS/EDGE (2006)	
Somtel Int'l	Somaliland only	GSM 900/1800 (2010) GPRS/EDGE (2011)	
Golis Telecoms	Puntland, Somaliland	GSM 900 (2005)	

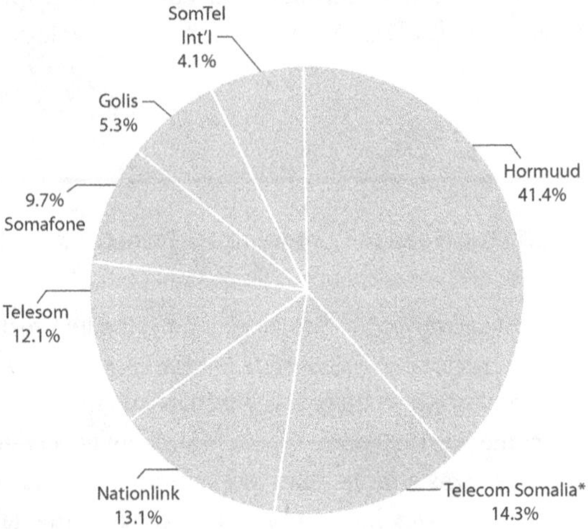

Pie chart — Estimated market shares: SomTel Int'l 4.1%, Golis 5.3%, Hormuud 41.4%, Somafone 9.7%, Telesom 12.1%, Nationlink 13.1%, Telecom Somalia* 14.3%

Source: World Bank data.
*Note: Acquired by SomTel Int'l in August 2013

Box 5.2 Regulatory Uncertainty as the Enemy of Investment: The Case of South Sudan

The regularization of mobile licences is one of the key challenges facing the telecommunication sector in the new Republic of South Sudan (RoSS). There were five mobile operators in the country at the time of independence (in July 2011): three that had nationwide licenses (MTN, Zain, and Sudani, which closed operations in February 2013) issued by the government in Khartoum and two operators (Gemtel and Vivacell) with licenses issued by the Government of Southern Sudan (GoSS). Mutual recognition of these licenses was outlined by an agreement signed between the Government of National Unity (GoNU) and GoSS in 2007. It is reported that, in 2011, the GoSS sent out requests to operators requesting a fee of US$200m, later raised to US$500m, for licences to operate, but this provoked strong opposition from the operators. A World Bank benchmarking study of mobile licenses elsewhere in East Africa suggested a figure of around US$7m per license would be more reasonable.

As an interim solution, a letter from the Ministry of Telecommunications and Postal Services was sent out to operators allowing them to continue operations with their existing licenses until the end of 2013. But in order to raise investment funds from their parent

box continues next page

Box 5.2 Regulatory Uncertainty as the Enemy of Investment: The Case of South Sudan *(continued)*

companies or from commercial banks, for instance to invest in fiber-optic cable to provide international connectivity, or to establish more base stations in rural states, more certainty is required over their future regulatory status and the level of license fees. Further uncertainty was introduced by rumors that the government has licensed an additional mobile operator, or by an attempt by the government to prohibit the operators from building their own base stations and obliging them to buy base station capacity from a company to which it has awarded an exclusive, monopoly license. The civil war which broke out in South Sudan in December 2013 has further chilled private sector confidence in the country.

The lack of symmetry among licenses also causes problems. For instance, one of the operators reports that it is paying the same level of annual spectrum fees that it was doing when servicing the whole country, even though South Sudan's population is barely an eighth of the former Republic of Sudan. Another operator managed to negotiate a clause in its license that there would be no further regulatory fees in return for a one-off payment at the time of license amendment, even though the license now extends for a period of 35 years, after the initial 20 years. While issuing new licenses is a necessary step for the to-be-created national regulator, the lack of a level playing field will make this difficult to achieve as some operators will inevitably gain while others will lose.

The Role of Information and Communication Technologies in Postconflict Reconstruction
http://dx.doi.org/10.1596/978-1-4648-0074-0

CHAPTER 6

Afghanistan

6.1 Introduction

Afghanistan is one of the world's poorest countries, and has experienced many years of violent conflict. Continuous violence from 1979 until the end of the last century destroyed most of the country's infrastructure and left millions of its citizens in exile. The collapse of the Taliban regime in 2001 led to a new government in Kabul, and a reopening of Afghanistan to the world. However, insurgency has continued in several parts of the country and the government has continued to be dependent on external military and development support. Central and local government institutions remain fragile as the country seeks to move from conflict to postconflict status. With the withdrawal of international military support now imminent, Afghanistan needs faster solutions to tackle its internal problems.

On the road to development, Afghanistan faces challenges in many areas, including the communications sector. Nevertheless, since 2001, the country has seen significant progress in the growth of its infrastructure, and there have been improvements in the delivery of government services to citizens.

The information and communication technology (ICT) sector has played a significant part in this transition. The number of telephone lines in the country has grown from less than 20,000 in 2001 to close to 20 million today, in a population of about 30 million. The country is also connecting to global information networks in the Middle East and South and Central Asia and is benefiting from the development of a national fiber-optic backbone. More diverse, plural media and information sources are now available, though their sustainability remains questionable. This short report summarizes that experience. The document is also supported by a video file, prepared for this project, as part of the World Bank programme on ICTs in postconflict reconstruction.[1]

6.2 Afghanistan's ICT Sector: From 2001 to 2012

Since the fall of the Taliban regime, the country has seen tremendous growth compared to what it had before. The 20-year conflict had led to the degradation of the human and technological capacity in the Ministry of Communications and Information Technology (MCIT). There was little by way of a functioning ICT ecosystem as late as the early 2000s, after the collapse of the Taliban regime. Afghanistan had only 20,000 operational telephones in 2001, most of which were in Kabul. There was no international connectivity. In fact, many Afghans had to cross international boundaries to make international telephone calls. The erstwhile Ministry of Telecommunications had combined policy, regulatory operational functions in a bundle.

Today, development is showing positive trends. Apart from the rapid growth in mobile telephony, the public as well as the private sector in Afghanistan have been using ICTs in increasingly sophisticated ways. This change over the past ten years has provided Afghans with access to information, to financial and transactional services, and to new markets. The government, with support from the World Bank and United States Agency for International Development (USAID), has initiated a number of programmes to expand electronic and mobile government services to citizens. Private businesses have begun to offer services such as money transfer and bill payments, agricultural market price information, and health information services using mobile networks and devices.

Development particularly seems to be catching up with younger Afghans, who are more technologically aware. They have established innovative enterprises that make use of ICTs. ICT sector and related activities are estimated to have created about 100,000 direct and indirect jobs in the country. ICT-related services have also created new sources of employment for educated young people, for women (who were excluded from employment by the Taliban), and, for example through sale of airtime vouchers, for poorer social groups. Telecommunications has expanded access to services such as banking and government for some citizens, and helped raise revenues for the government, which is otherwise largely dependent on donor assistance.

These indicators point toward a positive growth pattern in economic reconstruction aided by ICT infrastructure. However, several challenges remain unsolved. The volatile security situation in the country, infrastructure problems including the lack of access to electricity in rural areas, and slow progress in improving education have constrained the development of physical and human networks, and the potential for enterprises that make use of ICTs. Conservative social norms influence access to communications and employment opportunities for many people, particularly women. Policy and regulatory initiatives could therefore stimulate further developmental gains while addressing some of the ongoing challenges facing the ICT sector in the country.

6.3 Recent Developments

Globally, the decade since 2001 has seen a major expansion in access to ICTs, leading to a widespread social and economic impact. Changes in information access, improvements in social ties among citizens, changes in the relationship between citizens and the state, and developments in the production, exchange, and consumption of goods and services are some of the positive impacts that have been attributed to ICTs.

Facilitating this growth has been expansion in mobile telephony and the Internet. The number of telephone subscriptions worldwide increased from 3.5 billion in 2005 to almost 7 billion in 2012, the growth resulting almost entirely from the expansion of mobile networks. The number of people using the Internet is estimated to have grown over the same period from just over 1 billion to around 2.3 billion. Even in conflict-affected states (as defined by the World Bank), the number of mobile telephone subscriptions increased from 90 million in 2007 to 258 million in 2013. Broadband networks now offer the prospect of a further step change in communications access, though they are still very poorly available in low-income countries.

Afghanistan's experience has reflected this global trend. The number of mobile telephone subscriptions has increased rapidly, from 145,000 in 2003 to over 18 million in 2012. The cost of using a mobile phone has also dropped significantly, with some calling plans now charging the equivalent of less than one U.S cent per minute, down from over 30 U.S cents per minute in 2003.[2]

A number of factors, including the enabling environment, the institutional framework for the sector, and changes in supply and demand for communications services have played an important part in shaping the way Afghanistan has responded to the changing information and communications environment.

The Government of Afghanistan established a policy and regulatory framework that enabled private participation and competition early in the reconstruction process. This allowed a number of local and international investors to set up mobile telephone networks and begin providing Internet services, bringing into Afghanistan experience from other developing countries and enabling the establishment of competitive markets for communications. Total private investment in the sector since 2001 has exceeded US$2 billion. By 2012, the country had four private national mobile telephone networks, one private fixed service provider in competition with the state-owned operator, and over 20 Internet Service Providers.

This approach to the sector has been supported by a business-friendly institutional framework within the MCIT as well as the Afghan Telecommunications Regulatory Authority (ATRA). A succession of technically aware ministers, supported by technocrats, has established a consistent, forward-looking vision of sector development, which has engaged the private sector in spite of the volatile security and investment environment. While there is a shortage of skilled personnel at lower levels, the growth- and competition-oriented approach of MCIT and, increasingly, ATRA has contributed significantly to the growth of the ICT sector despite security and governance concerns.

Demand for more communications services has also been high, rising from a very low base in 2001. Take-up of mobile telephony has been especially rapid, reaching over 21 million subscriptions in 10 years. In 2012, broadband wireless services including 3G entered the market.[3] The state-owned Afghan Telecom's satellite-based Village Communications Network (VCN) (see box 6.1) was set

The Role of Information and Communication Technologies in Postconflict Reconstruction
http://dx.doi.org/10.1596/978-1-4648-0074-0

Box 6.1 Afghanistan's Village Communications Network

The state-owned operator Afghan Telecom maintains a satellite-based community kiosk program called the Village Communications Network (VCN). The VCN system consists of terminals that can support voice telephony and basic data services, with terminals installed in over 800 villages across the country (see map B6.1.1).

The VCN programme operates as follows. Potentially interested operators may purchase a terminal from Afghan Telecom for the equivalent of US$2,000. Some operators (such as nonprofit organizations) use these terminals for their own communication needs, while others convert them to telecenters. MCIT estimates that over a million people have benefitted from access through the VCN system.

Map B6.1.1 Map of Approximate Village Communications Network Locations

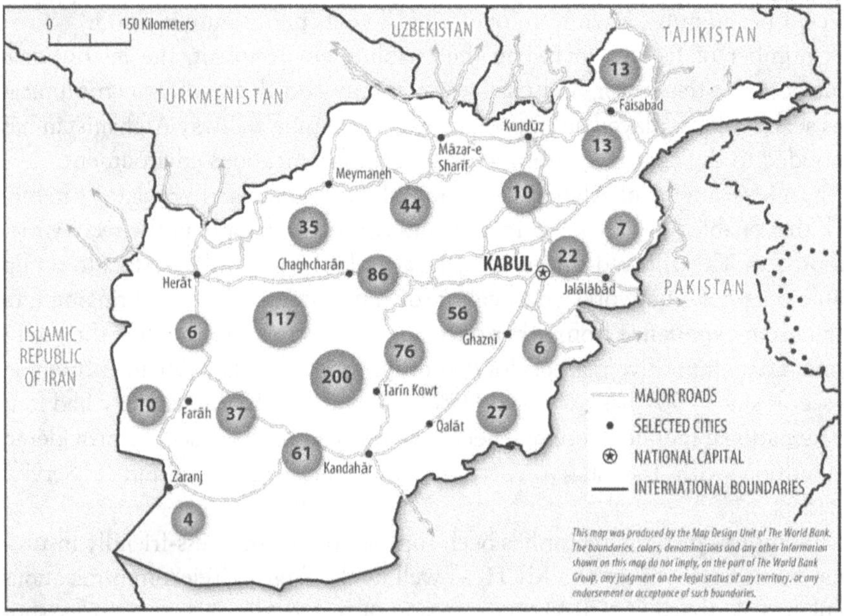

Source: World Bank based on MCIT; data
Note: Numbers represent the density of terminals in the area.

up in 2008. It attracted many potential small-scale entrepreneurs who were willing to invest the US$2,000 required to set up terminals and sell voice telephony in rural communities. A national survey in 2004 noted that more than half of households, including some in rural areas, had access to telephone services.[4] This experience is similar to that in other low-income developing countries. In Afghanistan, strong family ties between urban and rural areas and between those living in Afghanistan and the diaspora may have reinforced the demand for communications services.

The end of the Taliban regime has encouraged Afghans who left the country during the civil war to return home. Many of those returning have lived in countries where communications media are ubiquitous and the Internet and mobile telephony have become widespread. Their experience has fostered rapid diffusion of technology among middle-class and working families, especially in urban Afghanistan. Many of the ICT entrepreneurs who were responsible for setting up Internet facilities (including ISPs), software and web development firms, equipment shops, and repair centers, belong to the diaspora community. At the same time, many Afghan professionals were able to enter the public sector and civil service through lateral entry programmes. This created a group of competent and dynamic professionals working in the public sector.

The significant donor presence in Afghanistan has been another factor contributing to growth in ICTs. Some agencies, such as the World Bank, USAID, SIDA, and KOICA, have contributed directly to ICT sector development. Operational staff (including Afghans) working for these and other agencies have also used sophisticated ICTs in their workplaces, inspiring wider interest and use. Kabul today has many private IT skills training businesses. While the quality of these varies greatly, there is no doubt that the large number of students which they attract see IT skills as important in improving their employability.

Mobile application development is a further area of growth. Afghanistan now has a mobile-based social network, Paywast, with over 300,000 subscribers, close to the number of Facebook users in Afghanistan.[5] A number of government programmes are deploying mobile applications for project monitoring and service delivery. Mobile money services are also being used for private money transfers, bill payments, and government salary payments. As of 2012, some of these applications have moved beyond urban areas and are becoming available in rural communities. A government-wide mobile applications platform is in development. Experience in other countries suggests that mobile-based innovation can be a significant driver for entrepreneurship, jobs and firm creation. If the government, private sector, and individual innovators participate in this development, it is likely that Afghanistan can also benefit.

The extent to which this happens will depend substantially on the country's national and international connectivity. The government, led by MCIT, has promoted the development of a high-capacity fiber-optic backbone, the National Optical Ring Network, that will link all of the provinces within the country, as well as connecting Afghanistan with its six neighbors (Pakistan, China, Tajikistan, Uzbekistan, Turkmenistan, and Iran).

There is a major effort by the government to develop a high-capacity fiber-optic backbone network that could link the provinces and reconnect Afghanistan with the world. Some commentators are optimistic that this will enable Afghanistan to become an international transit hub for data within its region, drawing analogies with the historic 'Silk Route' trade route that ran through the country from ancient times. Whether it is able to capitalize on this depends on many factors, including the security situation, political relations with neighboring countries, and the development of those countries' own infrastructure and international transit capabilities.

6.4 Challenges to the Growth of the ICT Sector

Alongside these positive developments, there are many challenges to future growth of the ICT sector in Afghanistan, which illustrate the complex relationship between communications, development, and reconstruction. The continued violence which affects much of the country, already mentioned, presents high levels of risk and uncertainty for investors in all development sectors, including communications. The ICT sector has itself been a target. Five contract staff were killed and 20 injured during the construction of the national fiber-optic backbone. Since February 2008, mobile networks have regularly shut down their services at night to avoid attacks from criminal elements,[6] and towers are still attacked at times. Poor governance and the fragility of government institutions are further constraints. Corruption is widely acknowledged and needs to be addressed through the restructuring of governmental systems, processes, and norms. ICTs may contribute to this, as they have elsewhere, but cannot transform governance without political will and institutional reform.

Variations in income and literacy also pose a challenge to ICT sector development and the social and economic impact that technology might have. A skilled labor force is a necessary condition for the development of the ICT industry. Senior management in the country's telecommunications businesses is now largely Afghan. However, with only a handful of trained ICT engineers and technicians—many of them absorbed into government, donor agencies, or larger firms and contractors—there is less chance of vibrant ICT entrepreneurship and innovation emerging than has been the case in some other countries. Lack of skills among potential beneficiaries of ICTs, in a country with low levels of literacy, also poses challenges for those seeking to stimulate innovative service delivery. The country's infrastructure cannot currently support high technology approaches, such as multimedia interfaces, which need broadband networks. Alternative approaches, which are not bandwidth-intensive and use resources more readily available to the rural poor, are needed if ICTs are to improve access, overcome literacy barriers and disseminate information in the short to medium term. Strategic approaches to the evolution of networks and services have proved successful in other countries, from the Republic of Korea to China, and may offer lessons for Afghanistan.

6.5 Critical Issues to be Addressed

Three issues in particular need to be addressed if Afghanistan is to take full advantage of the opportunities which ICTs now make available.

Firstly, while much of the telecommunications sector has been privatized and liberalized, there are some remaining state monopolies. Private mobile and Internet service providers, for example, are not fully allowed to construct their own wireline networks for local or national telecommunications. The state has complete control over wireline networks in the country. This restriction hampers the ability of private businesses to deploy networks in response to demand, and so constrains private investment. Its removal would deepen competition—and will be essential if fair competition is to ensue whenever the state-owned enterprise is privatized.

Secondly, there is insufficient skilled labor in the ICT sector. However promising the enabling environment is for them, ICT firms cannot expand without skilled workers. Technical education needs to be better aligned with and responsive to the needs of industry, preparing students with the soft skills needed to excel as innovators and businesspeople as well as with technical expertise. MCIT is currently piloting an IT skills development programme, with the World Bank's support, to test ways to create this skills base. Stronger relationships amongst ICT professionals, through social networks and associations, could also stimulate collaboration. ICT training provided to government officials in donor programmes can help to generate such networking, as can groups such as the National ICT Association of Afghanistan.

Thirdly, the Government of Afghanistan has limited institutional and human capacity to transform services and programme management through ICTs. While most government officials recognize the value of ICT-enabled services, few government institutions can adopt them quickly or have the capacity to respond to increased demand from citizens. As the mobile telephone becomes an increasingly important channel for communications between citizens and the government, it will be increasingly important for the government to build institutional capacity that enables it to respond quickly to changing demand. Without this, citizen frustration could diminish government credibility.

These challenges illustrate the complexities and difficulties which limit the pace and extent of change that can be achieved through ICTs in a low-income, conflict-affected country such as Afghanistan. Transformation takes time, and it will be a while before ICTs can be the true driving force to social and economic development. There is a need for careful analysis and strategic planning to ensure that the infrastructure, human and institutional capacity are all in place to deliver the changes that people seek and that can contribute to reconstruction and development.

6.6   Insights for Other Conflict-affected and Fragile Countries and States

As in every country, context is crucial to understanding the context and potential for ICTs in Afghanistan. Experience, including that from Afghanistan, cannot simply be transferred from one conflict-affected country to another. Yet, some insights may have value in other fragile and conflict-affected states. Policy makers, it is suggested, should:

The Role of Information and Communication Technologies in Postconflict Reconstruction
http://dx.doi.org/10.1596/978-1-4648-0074-0

- Draw on local strengths and concepts to create a vision for the sector, positioning the country in a global context and providing a framework to create buy-in among citizens and other stakeholders
- Establish, at an early stage, a policy and regulatory framework that enables competition, liberalizes the market, and offers stability to investors and service providers
- Focus on the development of an initial pool of talent drawn from universities and other training programmes, and leveraging the skills and experience of diaspora and migrant networks
- Identify sources of demand that could quickly establish nonreversible gains in the sector and anchor other developments (for example, ICT skills development, mobile applications)
- Ensure that public agencies build their human and institutional capacities in order to undertake the needed technological transformation and respond to increased demand for services from an ICT-aware population
- Seek support from donors early on both in the creation of the policy and regulatory environment and in helping to attract talented personnel through lateral entry and capacity building efforts.

The story of Afghanistan's ICT sector over the past decade has been one of significant growth in a highly challenging environment. The country has an opportunity to accelerate this growth and build on its success to facilitate economic transformation. Whether it can achieve this depends partly on continuing changes in and continued development of the ICT sector, but also on the country's overall progress from conflict and fragility to stability and growth.

Notes

1. The video is available at http://youtu.be/nEIeACyhUk4. It was produced by FKH Media, Afghanistan.
2. Data from MICT and Wireless Intelligence (2012).
3. http://www.bbc.co.uk/news/business-19975113.
4. http://asiafoundation.org/resources/pdfs/Surveybook2012web1.pdf.
5. Interview with Paywast.
6. http://arstechnica.com/gadgets/2008/02/taliban-wants-cell-phone-networks-shut-down-at-night/.

CHAPTER 7

Liberia

Liberia, in recent decades, has been a byword for violent conflict. In 1980, Africa's oldest nation-state—founded in 1847 by freed slaves and freeborn African-Americans—descended into more than 20 years of civil war as traditional power structures and relationships between ethnic groups disintegrated. The conflict was exceptionally brutal, noted for the exploitation of child soldiers, and spilled over into neighboring countries. It destroyed most of the country's education, health, and economic infrastructure. Many of Liberia's 4 million people fled, depriving it of skills and expertise.

A peace agreement, signed in 2003, led first to a period of transitional government and then in 2005 to a new administration headed by Africa's first elected woman president, Ellen Johnson Sirleaf. As might be expected, 20 years of civil war have left Liberia among the world's poorest countries, with gross national income of just US$240 in 2011. In spite of renewed economic growth since the peace agreement, Liberia is unlikely to meet the majority of MDGs by 2015. The country is highly dependent on international donors.

Liberia's fixed telecommunications infrastructure did not survive the civil war. There is, in practice, no fixed network in the country, but, as elsewhere in Africa, mobile telephony has been enthusiastically adopted by Liberians. Mobile networks, which in 2009 covered just 32 percent of the population, now cover the majority. Mobile teledensity rose from almost zero in 2000 to just under 40 percent in 2010: still not high by African standards but a great improvement in a very poor country.[1] Rates of computer and Internet participation, however, are very low. The World Bank and ITU estimated PC ownership in 2010 at just over 1 percent of the population, and just 7 percent of Liberians were estimated to have meaningful access to the Internet.

In spite of these low levels of adoption, information and communication technology (ICTs) featured prominently in the government's first Poverty Reduction Strategy (2008–11), and this has been reinforced by a National ICT and Telecommunications Policy which was agreed in 2010.[2] The Policy stresses the importance of broadband deployment as a driver for the ICT sector and value-added services. Achieving this requires attention to international connectivity, the national backbone and local access.

The study of Liberia undertaken for this World Bank programme focused on three different aspects of the country's recent experience of ICTs and their value in postconflict reconstruction. These are:

- Arrangements for connecting Liberia to international submarine cables, an essential part of enabling the country to take advantage of broadband applications
- The use of cybercafés, an important part of Internet access for citizens in-country
- The website that contributed to the work of the country's Truth and Reconciliation Commission.

Although not comprehensive, these illustrative case studies, each of which is essentially a stand-alone report, contribute toward an overall picture of the role which ICTs are playing in postconflict Liberia.

7.1 Submarine Cable Connectivity

By 2012, Liberia was one of very few countries in the world that was not connected to international submarine optic fiber cables, but reliant still on slower, more expensive satellites for international connectivity. The country was embroiled in conflict and unable to participate when the SAT-3 cable was laid at the turn of the century, with landing points in most other West African countries. The cost of using satellites—some US$3000 per Mbps per month, about 10 times that of cable connectivity—has inhibited access to international data, including the Internet, and curtailed economic opportunities. Not surprisingly, therefore, gaining access to submarine cable was a central objective of the national ICT strategy agreed in 2010, alongside the development of a national backbone network and improvements in local connectivity throughout the country. Aspirations for cable connectivity are high, in terms of economic growth and employment opportunity, improvements in government administration and services, and unlocking innovative potential in the country's population.

The opportunity to connect to cable emerged in 2010, when France Télécom-Orange initiated the ACE (African Coast to Europe) project to compete with the existing SAT-3 and Main One cables along an 18-country route between Europe and South Africa. The ACE consortium now consists of 16 businesses, including France Télécom and national network operators in countries along its route.

Liberia's state-owned network operator, Libtelco, and its national communications regulator, the Liberia Telecommunications Authority (LTA), were both unable to secure private capital to support participation in the consortium. Addressing this investment challenge, the World Bank provided over $20 million of capital and technical assistance to enable a public-private partnership to participate, through a special purpose vehicle called the Cable Consortium of Liberia (CCL). This consortium includes the government and two private network operators. World Bank support in Liberia forms part of the first phase of the West African Regional Communications Infrastructure Program (WARCIP), which also supports telecoms development in a neighboring country, Sierra Leone, itself recovering from protracted civil war. CCL is owned 60 percent by the Government of Liberia, 20 percent by Libtelco and 10 percent each by two private operators, Cellcom and MTN's Lone Star Communications. The ACE cable landed in Liberia in late 2011. It became operational over part of its course in December 2012.

The study of the consortium undertaken for this programme focused on institutional arrangements and decision making concerning Liberia's involvement. These involved a number of government agencies, private companies, and international development partners, as illustrated in figure 7.1.

As noted above, CCL was established because it proved impossible for either the state-owned telco or the regulator to secure sufficient private capital for participation. CCL has signed a construction and maintenance agreement with the ACE consortium which gives it authority to design and manage the cable landing station in Liberia and to allocate capacity to its shareholders. Technically, CCL is a contractual agreement rather than a partnership, and so the benefits arising from participation in it are proportionate to each party's level of ownership.

Figure 7.1 Structure of the Consortium Created to Invest in the ACE Cable, Liberia

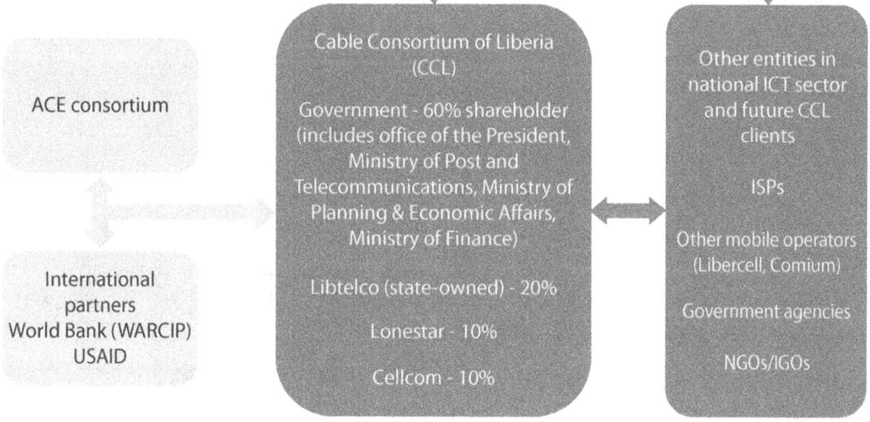

Source: World Bank data.
Note: ACE = African Coast to Europe; CCL = Cable Consortium of Liberia; ICT = information and communication technology; ISP = Internet service provider; NGO = nongovernmental organization; LTA = Liberian Telecommunication Authority; USAID = United States Agency for International Development; WARCIP = West African Regional Communications Infrastructure Program.

Decision making within CCL does not entirely follow this balance-of-owner-ship arrangement. The government appoints only one of five directors of the consortium, though two more are appointed by Libtelco, so that there is poten-tially a government majority. Relationships between shareholders are complicat-ed by historic disputes between them. The regulator LTA has been designated as an independent intermediary between the shareholders should one be required.

Some questions arise from CCL's status as a special purpose vehicle—usually a temporary measure, rather than a more lasting public-private partnership (PPP). CCL is also unusual, as a PPP, in that the majority of funding is provided by the government, through World Bank financing. There has been some concern that the benefits derived by government from its shareholding may make it less inclined to divest its holding in the consortium or privatize Libtelco in due course.

Relationships within CCL and between it and the rest of the ICT community will strongly influence the value of cable connectivity to Liberia's development. Experience elsewhere has shown that access to international bandwidth for non-members of cable consortia is critical to the price of Internet access. Open access rules have been incorporated in CCL's shareholder agreement, including a requirement to sell commercial services to nonmembers of the consortium on a nondiscriminatory basis—though (as yet unspecified) "reasonable preference" may be afforded to shareholders.

In all these processes, a relatively small number of elite personnel can be iden-tified as taking a crucial role in decision making, including the commissioners of LTA and the managing director of Libtelco. Although formal decision making was influenced by the World Bank and other technical agencies, individual per-sonalities played a significant role in informal bargaining around the terms and conditions of participation in CCL and so in ACE. The significance of these personalities should not be underestimated.

The cable project has strong support within the Government of Liberia, which hopes to take advantage of increased bandwidth as it rolls out a compre-hensive government network to improve administration and service delivery. Political support for the cable has come from political opponents as well as gov-ernment supporters, and there has been little criticism in the media. Even VSAT operators, which might be expected to lose out once ACE comes into operation, have been supportive, seeing continued opportunities both in the transition period and beyond, as failsafe connectivity suppliers in the event of cable failure. The LTA is planning a series of consultation processes which, it is hoped, will maintain public support for the cable venture as well as helping to direct the course of telecommunications services.

Past mistrust between operators within the sector, and between operators and the regulator, is one cause of concern. Collaboration between these entities is not only important where CCL is concerned. It will also be critical in maximizing the value of cable connectivity as the national backbone network is developed. One important part of national infrastructure, for example, which requires collabora-tion across the sector is the establishment of an Internet Exchange Point (IXP), which would enable national Internet traffic to be routed locally rather than over international networks.

The LTA is charged both with regulating the sector and with securing the necessary collaboration between stakeholders. Unfortunately it has not yet fully developed a strong position within the industry and has struggled to establish its authority over mobile operators, for example in disputes over interconnection, spectrum interference, and the colocation of facilities. While telecommunications operators are among the country's largest companies, exerting significant economic power, the regulator has been constrained by a lack of technical and human resources to carry out its functions.

Lack of technical expertise and enforcement capacity are problems that will continue to face the LTA in managing its responsibilities. Liberians have little experience in creating or maintaining the necessary infrastructure and have relied on support from the World Bank and USAID. The multidonor Public-Private Infrastructure Advisory Facility (PPIAF) has been providing expertise since 2007. Foreign expatriates are expected to continue playing an important role, often tied to donor funding. The government needs to determine how best to transfer these roles to domestic personnel and build the necessary expertise.

It is worth noting that World Bank support for the project was not always certain. The bank had reservations about the involvement of Libtelco before privatization, while the Government of Liberia preferred to improve the national operator's market and financial position prior to sale. The WARCIP loan through which the bank supports participation in ACE comes in three components, the largest (initial) component including the consortium fee, while later tranches cover policy support and project implementation (with a bank unit based at LTA).

The study's overview of this experience juxtaposes institutional, technical, and political factors. Several recommendations follow from its analysis. In a complex arrangement such as this PPP, for example, care needs to be taken to protect against corruption in procurement. The Government of Liberia is encouraged to plan ahead for the sale of its share in CCL, and to facilitate participation by the diaspora. The success of the whole venture will depend substantially on LTA's ability to intermediate between operators, ensuring nondiscrimination while improving its own capabilities. It will be important to balance different interests, formal and informal. The experience illustrates many of the challenges of governance faced by postconflict administrations, concerning ICTs and other policy domains.

International connectivity obviously has little value without ongoing connectivity in-country. Further support from WARCIP is therefore available for a universal access fund, which will also benefit in due course from sale of the government's shares in CCL. Universal access funds in other countries have not always focused on the needs of marginalized users, and the World Bank is keen to ensure that this one does. Consultation by LTA should play an important part in targeting resources, while the government should take the opportunity to enhance domestic expertise as the national backbone project is planned and implemented.

The Role of Information and Communication Technologies in Postconflict Reconstruction
http://dx.doi.org/10.1596/978-1-4648-0074-0

7.2 Cybercafé Users in Liberia

The second study of ICTs in Liberia, undertaken for this World Bank programme makes use of a survey of cybercafé users in Liberia's capital Monrovia. One hundred users were interviewed at four locations in greater Monrovia during December 2011. Informants were interviewed as they left cybercafés and rewarded for their help with Internet access time. Interviews focused on their usage patterns and motivations.

Internet use in Liberia is low, estimated at just 7 percent of the population in 2010 but growing rapidly from that low base. Mobile access to the Internet is likely to be growing fast, as it is elsewhere in Africa, but no figures for this are yet available. At the time of the study, even for wealthier Liberians, cybercafés were the principal means of personal access to the Internet.

Cybercafé use in Liberia is not evenly spread across the population, but is commonest among younger men. 90 percent of informants were male, and just over 50 percent aged between 25 and 34. The interview sample was highly educated, with all informants reporting secondary education and 76 percent having a college degree. Average reported income, at $300 p.m., was ten times higher than the average in Liberia. Over 40 percent of informants said that they were self-employed.

Most of the sample also had substantial computer skills, over 90 percent reporting more than three years' computer experience, 80 percent more than three years' Internet experience, and the large majority considering their skills to be good or very good, reflecting experience of the Internet and more complex computing activities.

Most informants engaged in a number of Internet activities during each visit to the cybercafé. As indicated in figure 7.2, the most significant activities were interactive communications (email, social networking, and IM chat) and browsing.

High-bandwidth entertainment applications such as watching movies, gaming, and downloading music were not commonly accessed, and there was a very low level of e-commerce activity, reflecting the limited range of e-commerce available in-country. The study's authors suggest that the focus on instrumental

Figure 7.2 Popular Cybercafé Applications in Liberia

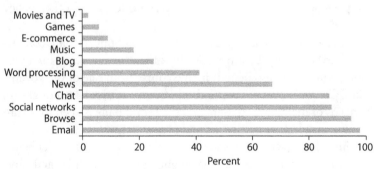

Source: World Bank data.

The Role of Information and Communication Technologies in Postconflict Reconstruction
http://dx.doi.org/10.1596/978-1-4648-0074-0

activities this reveals may reflect the country's "conflict-stressed, low-resource, and low-bandwidth environment."

In analysing these results, the study identifies three clusters of users, based on the basket of services that they employ while at the cybercafé:

- A majority that, on each visit makes use of the most commonly accessed services (email, browsing, networking, and IM chat, described as the "usual services")
- A smaller group of basic service users, mostly concerned with email and browsing
- A sophisticated user group that makes use of the "usual services" but also blogs and may use e-commerce sites.

These different patterns of use are illustrated in figure 7.3.

Sophisticated users, as identified here, were much more likely to have access to a computer at home than other informants.

The most significant purposes of Internet use reported by respondents were interactive communications activities (69 percent), followed by education (54 percent) and income-related activities (36 percent). This last activity area was more likely to be concerned with job-seeking than with product or client search. The emphasis on interactive uses that this reveals is widespread in Africa and elsewhere, though the study suggests that it may also reflect a slowly developing postconflict environment.

Most respondents felt that their cybercafé use was positive for themselves and their family, though some felt it had negative impacts on friends and families. Sophisticated users, as identified above, were more likely, and basic users less likely, to have positive overall assessments of their cybercafé activity.

Many of the respondents to the survey regarded the Internet as their main information source, for example for world news but also for educational purposes, as indicated in figure 7.4. Radio was also popular amongst these informants, but less so than the Internet, and newspapers were significant for job and business, government, and health information. (The high education and income profiles of the informant group, relative to Liberians as a whole, should be borne

Figure 7.3 Cybercafé Usage Patterns in Liberia

Source: World Bank data.

The Role of Information and Communication Technologies in Postconflict Reconstruction
http://dx.doi.org/10.1596/978-1-4648-0074-0

Figure 7.4 Reliance on the Internet for Different Sources of Information, Liberia

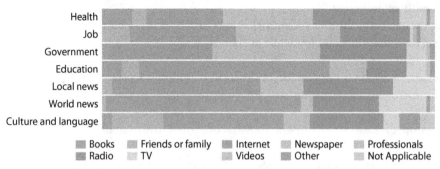

Source: World Bank data.

Figure 7.5 Reliance on Different ICTs for Information, Liberia

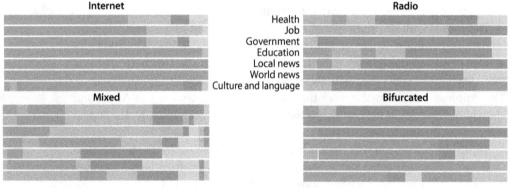

Source: World Bank data.

in mind here—as should the fact that cybercafés are a minority mode of information access. For the population as a whole, radio is much more significant.)

Analysis of these results shows that about a third of informants were very highly reliant on the Internet for the types of information described in figure 7.4. Around 40 percent used a mix of different information sources, while two smaller groups could be identified: one consisting of those who were most dependent on radio, and another, described as "bifurcated" users, who relied predominantly on radio for some purposes and the Internet for others. These categories are illustrated in figure 7.5.

Not surprisingly, it was "sophisticated users" who were most likely to be highly reliant on the Internet as their primary information source, as well as to report positive impacts from their Internet experience. Nine of the sample's 100 informants fell into this category, all but one of whom were male. These sophisticated users did not show any particular demographic distinctiveness from others in the sample, other than the likelihood that they also made use of computers in the home. All had at least three years' experience of computers and the Internet, and most described their skills as good rather than very good, suggesting that they aspire to additional skills.

The Role of Information and Communication Technologies in Postconflict Reconstruction
http://dx.doi.org/10.1596/978-1-4648-0074-0

Although the sample size is small, the study authors consider it sufficient to suggest that the survey reveals a small group of young, savvy, technologically optimistic, and aspirational individuals, which it describes as "super-techies," similar to those found in other conflict-stressed situations such as countries that have experienced the Arab Spring, and in countries such as Kenya and Nigeria. It suggests that this has implications for initiatives led by governments or international organizations that require local expertise, indicating a potential for locally led innovation in the economy, and suggesting the value of nurturing a local pool of talent and skills in the Liberian ICT sector. More evidence is needed to corroborate this finding.

7.3 Reconciliation and the Web

The third study of Liberia in the World Bank programme concerns the use of the World Wide Web within the work of Liberia's Truth and Reconciliation Commission (TRC). The study provides an account of this by authors who were directly involved in developing the Commission's website and related services. Their experience provides a case study of the use of Internet in TRC processes which may have relevance for other postconflict environments.

Truth and reconciliation commissions, the best known of which followed the end of apartheid in South Africa, are vehicles through which people in a society can together investigate the history and nature of their country's conflict, allowing all parties to testify about their experience. Overall goals of such commissions include acknowledging and addressing the needs of victims, promoting accountability and helping societies toward a measure of "closure." They usually hold public hearings as well as collecting private testimony, and conclude with a published report. Although they may complement conventional legal processes, they are not usually located within the formal justice system. Worldwide, more than 40 countries have now implemented such commissions.

Liberia's TRC was mandated in the 2003 peace agreement and implemented following legislation in 2005. Its remit include the investigation of human rights violations, causes of the conflict, the exploitation of natural resources and the experiences of women and children during the period 1979–2003. It was required to provide opportunities for victims and perpetrators, both in-country and in the diaspora, to express their views and describe their experiences. In all it received some 20,000 statements during its work, before submitting its final report in 2009.

Although some—surprisingly not all—TRCs have used the Web to disseminate material about themselves and publish their reports, none before Liberia's had used the Internet to gather submissions or allow users to interact with content, and almost none had offered multimedia features such as video. Liberia's was therefore one of the first to make use of the Internet's interactive capabilities.

Work to develop the Liberian TRC's website was commissioned in 2007 from the United States university the Georgia Institute of Technology (Georgia Tech). Given the Internet's very limited reach in Liberia, it was evident that a conventional Web presence, however interactive, would only be accessible to a limited user base within Liberia, but would be more accessible to Liberians in the diaspora and to the international community. Georgia Tech personnel therefore worked with members of the diaspora in their local area, in a participatory process, to design and develop a new website which would be perceived as relevant by Liberians. Design and content development emphasized themes of truth, forgiveness, justice, reconciliation, safety, and security. The website was also designed to include multimedia content—photographs, video, and audio—and to offer interactive services such as discussion spaces, the opportunity to contact commissioners, and—a first for any TRC—to submit sworn testimony over the Internet. The final home page for the site is illustrated in figure 7.6.

Following its launch in early 2008, the site received some 2,500 unique visitors each month, rising during the Commission's hearings to a peak of almost 11,000 in the month that its final report was published, November 2009. User numbers fell back to around 1,000 a month following publication.

Figure 7.6 Website of the Liberia Truth and Reconciliation Commission

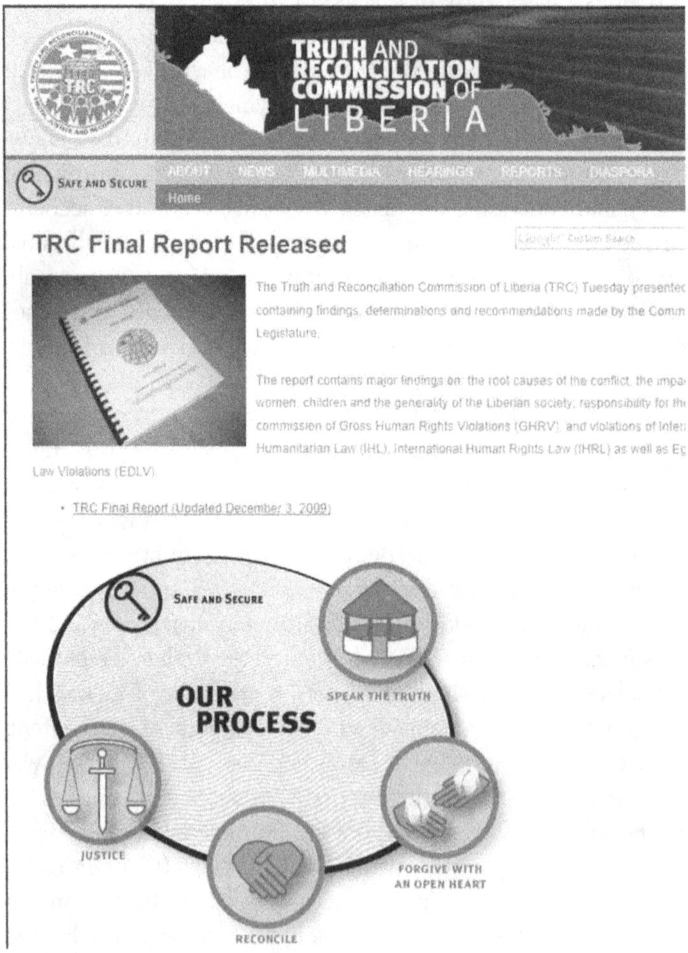

Source: www.trcofliberia.org

It is difficult to locate the origin of visitors to the site, as international traffic routing means that traffic originating in Liberia may be logged as originating in North America. Even so, the data suggest that a high proportion of traffic derived from the diaspora.

The most popular section of the site was that providing the opportunity for users to search video content. About 1,000 videos were made available, nearly all of these documenting public hearings conducted by the Commission. The download page for the Commission's final report was also popular, as was content summarizing the Commission's work. Discussion fora and interactive pages which allowed visitors to contribute their own material, however, received very few visits compared with the multimedia content that was made available. This contrasts with the enthusiasm with which Liberians in rural areas contributed their views and experiences—often on current issues rather than past conflict—in travelling kiosks which gathered evidence for the Commission.[3]

The study's authors, who were responsible for website development, identify three findings from this experience. They believe that it reinforced the importance of participatory design, including Liberians in the diaspora as well as those living in-country; of emphasizing processes of reconciliation rather than the institutional character of the Commission; and of providing rich media content in supporting truth and reconciliation.

7.4 Conclusion

The study of Liberia reported in this chapter draws attention to three aspects of ICTs in a low-income country which has experienced prolonged civil conflict. It suggests ways in which ICTs can be used to contribute to reconciliation processes, and ways in which individuals are developing skills, through personal use of computers and the Internet, that could have lasting developmental value. The opportunity to leverage these opportunities depends substantially, however, on the ability of governments and the private sector to enable reliable, affordable connectivity to international bandwidth, within the country and in local communities. The quality of government decision making on the ICT and other sectors is also important to this. These findings are considered further in Part 1 of the report.

Notes

1. Michael L. Best et al. reports mobile usage charges as "reputedly the lowest in West Africa": "Uses of Mobile Phones in Post-Conflict Liberia," in *Proceedings of the 3rd international conference on Information and communication technologies and development*, 2010, pp. 468–77.

2. Government of Liberia, Ministry of Posts and Telecommunications, 2010, "National ICT and Telecommunications Policy."

3. This experience is reported in Thomas N. Smyth et al. 2010. "MOSES—Exploring New Ground in Media and Post-Conflict Reconciliation," in *Proceedings of the SIGCHI Conference on Human Factors in Computing Systems*, pp. 1059–68.

The Role of Information and Communication Technologies in Postconflict Reconstruction
http://dx.doi.org/10.1596/978-1-4648-0074-0

CHAPTER 8

Rwanda

Rwanda, a country of 11.5 million people in central Africa, experienced repeated ethnic conflict in the decades following independence in 1962, culminating in genocide, civil war, and rebel victory in 1994. Within three months that year, between 500,000 and 1 million Rwandans were killed, the government was overthrown by rebel forces, and hundreds of thousands more people left the country. The resulting humanitarian crisis and its legacy are still felt throughout Central Africa, though there has been no resurgence of violence in Rwanda itself since 1994.

The period since then, under the presidency of Paul Kagame, has seen considerable economic recovery and growth. Annual growth in gross domestic product (GDP) has been around 7 percent in recent years and the incidence of poverty fell by some 12 percent between 2006 (56.7 percent) and 2011 (44.9 percent). The country is approaching average levels for low-income countries in indicators including gross national income (GNI) *per capita* and life expectancy at birth. Progress in education has been widely commended, with primary school enrolment well above the average in Sub-Saharan Africa and planned reforms in secondary education. The environment for business has improved rapidly, with the country now 52nd in the World's Bank *Doing Business* index. Rwanda has been a major recipient of international development assistance since 1994.

Since the 1990s, the Government of Rwanda has placed particular emphasis on the developmental role and potential of information and communication technologies (ICTs), implementing a series of planned phases of work which are described in this chapter. While these have achieved significant gains, important challenges remain, within the sector and more broadly.

Rwanda's experience, reviewed in this chapter, offers a valuable case study of ICTs in development, both within and beyond postconflict reconstruction. The chapter begins by briefly summarizing *Vision 2020*, the government's overall development strategy which has set ambitious goals to achieve middle-income status for the country. Closely connected with this has been a succession of four National Information and Communication Infrastructure (NICI) plans. These have sought to reform the ICT sector through privatization and liberalization, infrastructure deployment, and ICT-enabled development initiatives in a variety of sectors. Finally, the chapter describes four specific ICT projects. The Karisimbi Project is an example of infrastructural development concerned with connectivity; the World Bank-funded eRwanda program has provided expertise and supported particular connectivity and productivity gains; TRACnet is an example of the use of technology to improve healthcare; while the One Laptop Per Child (OLPC) programme is an attempt to improve educational performance through provision of low-cost computers.

Neither the strategies nor the specific programmes described here have been without their problems, and ICTs have certainly not proved to be a cure-all in postconflict Rwanda. However, the manner in which the strategy has been implemented—with high-level support—offers a valuable experience from which other developing and postconflict countries can draw lessons.

8.1 Policy and Implementation

8.1.1 Vision 2020

Rwanda has sought to rebuild its economy and society in the face of multiple challenges arising from historically low levels of development, its landlocked status, and the legacy of conflict. The new political leadership that took power in 1994 recognized that the traditional agricultural sector would not generate sufficient economic and employment growth, and introduced a new development framework, *Vision 2020*. This aimed to set Rwanda on a path "from a subsistence agriculture economy to a knowledge-based society, with high levels of savings and private investment." While *Vision 2020* has evolved over time, its core goal has remained the same: to transform Rwanda into a middle-income country, embracing inclusive growth and political stability. The targets for *Vision 2020* (see Figure 8.1) were upgraded in 2012. It now seeks to achieve GDP of US$1,240 *p.c.* (previously US$900) and a ceiling of 20 percent living below the poverty line (previously 30 percent).

Vision 2020 builds on six pillars, through which government aims to create a favorable environment for private sector investment, not least in infrastructure and human resources. ICTs are expected to play a multilayered and cross-cutting role in its achievement—from basic infrastructure to support for education and business development.

Within *Vision 2020*, strategies for Rwanda's ICT sector have been set out in four successive National Information and Communication Infrastructure (NICI) plans. These plans—each spanning five of the twenty years of *Vision 2020*—have guided government efforts to reform and improve the ICT sector.

8.1.2 NICI-1

NICI-1 (the plan for 2001–05) focused on institutional and policy structures for future ICT growth. During this period, the government undertook a process of privatization and market liberalization, resulting in the establishment of two mobile network operators—Rwandatel and MTN-owned Rwandacell—and

Figure 8.1 National Information & Communication Infrastructure Plans (NICIs), Rwanda

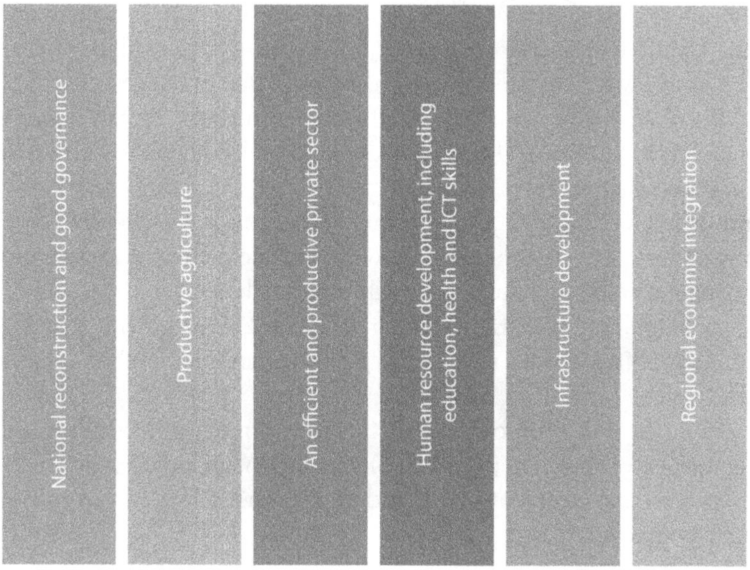

Source: World Bank data.

three Internet Service Providers. Management of the ICT sector was delegated to the Rwandan Utilities Regulatory Authority (RURA) and the Rwandan Information Technology Authority (RITA). The National Information Technology Commission (NITC) was set up to serve as an advisory group and think-tank. Finally, a universal service fund was established to promote access to rural and poorer communities, with finance derived from operator turnover. Specific infrastructural investments in the plan included a 150-kilometre fiber-optic network in the capital Kigali. Efforts to boost ICT skills were promoted through the a national training center at the Kigali Institute of Science & Technology (KIST) and ICT training at the National University.

This policy framework was well regarded by donors and other governments in Africa. However, ICT indicators showed little progress during the plan period. By 2005, fixed line penetration was stuck at 0.3 percent, mobile penetration had only risen to 2.5 percent, and just 0.6 percent of the population was using the Internet. The government conceded that plan implementation had suffered from deficiencies in infrastructure and human resources, with both government officials and the general public showing low-ICT awareness and readiness.

8.1.3 NICI-2

The country's second ICT plan, NICI-2, set out the policy focus for the next five years, 2005–10. It allocated US$500 million across 10 thematic areas—from infrastructure and rural access to social and economic development, from policy and regulation to private sector development and human capacity building, and from national security to education and e-government. Activities in this period included upgrading national ICT infrastructure, a national identity smartcard, a national data center, and improved access to international bandwidth. In Kigali, the municipal government partnered with RURA, the Rwanda Development Board, and the Ministry of Infrastructure to pilot wireless broadband. Improved access to information was supported through the World Bank-financed eRwanda programme (described below). Market liberalization also continued: in 2009, a third mobile operator, Millicom/Tigo, joined the market, leading to lower tariffs and growth in subscriber numbers.

By the end of NICI-2, many ICT indicators pointed in a positive direction. The most obvious success was the growth of mobile telephony and Internet uptake, following increased investment, though this paralleled growth elsewhere in Africa and so should not be attributed entirely to the Plan. By 2011, Rwanda had 11 ISPs, 700,000 internet users, and nearly 6 million mobile phone subscriptions.

Nevertheless, in its evaluation of NICI-2, the Government of Rwanda again highlighted a number of shortcomings in implementation, including weaknesses in leadership, project management and coordination, and a lack of systematic monitoring and evaluation.

8.1.4 NICI-3

The third NICI plan, which runs until 2015, was adopted by the government in early 2011. While its predecessors focused on policy and infrastructure, NICI-3 concentrates on ICT service delivery, targeting local communities more directly. Its five central objectives are concerned with skills, community development, private sector development in the ICT sector, cybersecurity, and e-government. These are no longer described as pillars or thematic areas, but as "clusters." The change in terminology reflects lessons learnt from NICI-1 and NICI-2 whose implementation is felt to have been insufficiently flexible, with too little interaction and cooperation between different pillars. As a result, NICI-3 will be implemented by cluster groups of experts, working to two-year implementation frameworks and exploring synergies across their different areas of responsibility.

Details of projects included in the clusters can be found in the NICI-3 plan. Emphasis is given in this to capacity development in local and rural communities and among individual users, including distance learning. This is believed to enhance the private sector development component, as surveys have indicated that lack of qualified ICT staff has held back growth. The private sector will also be supported through electronic payment systems, improved access to finance, and entrepreneurial and business training for ICT providers.

8.1.5 NICI-4

The fourth plan, NICI-4, will consolidate the entire NICI process after 2015, as the overall *Vision 2020* reaches its target date. By that time, the government hopes, the NICIs will have helped to turn Rwanda into "an information-rich knowledge-based society and economy" whose key sectors have been modernized by ICTs, fulfilling the objectives described in the *Vision* document. It remains to be seen if Rwanda can achieve these ambitions in practice.

The Role of Information and Communication Technologies in Postconflict Reconstruction
http://dx.doi.org/10.1596/978-1-4648-0074-0

8.2 Project Case Studies

A wide range of government-led or -coordinated information and communications for development (ICT4D) projects has been implemented in Rwanda since 1995. In line with NICI plans described above, these initially focused on establishing an enabling environment for ICTs, including education and human resource development as well as physical infrastructure such as fiber and transmission towers. Many initiatives have addressed a combination of infrastructure, content, and applications. Four projects that have had significant impact on Rwanda's approach are outlined in the following paragraphs, illustrating different ways in which ICTs have been incorporated in the country's development strategy.

8.2.1 *The Karisimbi Project*

The Government of Rwanda has sought to improve access to communications for rural communities as part of *Vision 2020*. Mount Karisimbi, the country's highest point, has been the focus of one notable government-funded infrastructure project—the construction of a 50-metre telecommunication mast on its summit, connected to the national optic fiber backbone.

This project had multiple goals:

- To facilitate cheap and effective communication access in both rural and urban areas
- To enhance cell phone coverage and access to TV and radio
- To establish an infrastructure hub for mobile Internet and mobile broadband access, with an open access approach to interconnection with network providers
- To support electronic applications such as virtual tourism, e-learning, e-health, e-commerce, e-government, and the tracking of goods along supply chains
- To bolster broadcasting capacity, including digital broadcasting
- To collect data for meteorology and disaster management
- To introduce an air safety, surveillance, and traffic management system.

It was hoped that the Karisimbi Project would reduce the cost of communication in Rwanda by about 50 percent on average. Although a pillar of national infrastructure investment—the first FM antenna was installed on the mountain in the 1980s—the project has faced significant obstacles and delays as a result of lack of electrification and poor coordination among construction teams. One positive outcome of the project has been the choice of Rwanda as host of a regional air traffic surveillance center, backed with a $8.6 million grant to the Karisimbi Project by the African Development Bank. Completed in late 2011, the long-term impact of the project is yet to be assessed.

8.2.2 *eRwanda*

eRwanda is a $10 million programme funded by the World Bank, at the request of the Government of Rwanda, as a core component of NICI-2. This project was the first ICT stand-alone project in Rwanda. It aimed to improve both the efficiency and effectiveness of targeted internal government processes, and the delivery of services in selected sectors, by enhancing access to information through the use of new technology. The project was aligned with the National Development Strategy (*Vision 2020*) and the NICI plans described above. The eRwanda project focused on the core activities ofNICI-2, including the development of an e-government platform and applications, funding support to build ICT infrastructure in government offices, and the establishment of an environment conducive to ICT sector development and increased ICT awareness among citizens.

The project disbursed US$10m before its closure in December 2012, in the following areas of activity:

- ICT infrastructure in government offices (PC, printers, IT equipment, Internet, Local and Wide Area Networks)
- e-Government applications (eCabinet, eParliament)
- Websites for ministries and government agencies in Kinyarwanda, the national language
- Telecenters and ICT buses (mobile telecenters)
- The eSoko project
- Telemedicine
- ICT skills training for government officials and citizens
- A capacity building programme for monitoring and evaluation at local university level, including the use of surveys to measure user perceptions (see Box 8.1).

The ICT platform developed through this project can be adjusted to improve the delivery of government social and economic services, and to improve the ICT awareness and capabilities of the population. It has enabled the government to connect with a larger number of citizens, including those in remote areas, and to deliver information more effectively and flexibly. It has trained around 2,800 people in basic ICT literacy, including 800 women and girls, and helped rural businesses to improve their supply chain management.

Box 8.1 Women's Networking for Peace Using ICTs

Peace X Peace is an international women's peace organization that uses technology tools to connect women in different cultures to provide mutual support and concerted action through "women's circle relationships" and "sister to sister relationships." These are intended to reduce barriers arising from linguistic and cultural differences, intolerance and conflict. Technology tools used include Drupal, CiviCRM, and Roundpoint's Cerkle platform, which hosts the project's Global Network. This is a secure, profile-based matching system that connects individual women and groups into egalitarian online circles.

The technology platform helps members connect, build mutual support, advocate for change and mobilize to take action. Nearly 20,000 members in more than 100 countries,

---

box continues next page

Box 8.1 Women's Networking for Peace Using ICTs *(continued)*

connected through personal computers or mobile phones, participate in programmes that highlight women's peace-building activities, promote women's leadership in peace process-es, and promote specific peace actions at multiple levels and in multiple languages (remov-ing language barriers for English, Arabic, Spanish, and French speakers with real-time message translation). Women in remote locations or those without access to computers can participate through cell phones. The website allows women to highlight stories from the frontlines of conflict and engages and connects women peace builders though their virtual classroom, a multimedia archive, blogs, and best-practice resources for women's circles and connections. Their technology approach helps their members overcome linguistic, geo-graphic, political, and cultural isolation to connect for peace building.

Source: Peace X Peace: Connecting Women for Peace, http://www.peacexpeace.org/content/, cited in Melhem et al. (2007).

8.2.3 TRACnet

TRACnet is an integrated ICT system to facilitate antiretroviral therapy (ART) for AIDS/HIV patients. It connects health clinics which are responsible for ART with central institutions including the government's Centre for Treatment and Research on AIDS, Malaria, Tuberculosis and other Epidemics (TRAC Plus), the National Laboratory, and CAMERWA, a pharmaceutical company administering ART drug stocks across the country.

In ART, it is critical that patients take medication regularly and that progress is closely monitored. After as little as 30 minutes' training, local healthcare work-ers can use a computer or mobile phone to report patient data and requirements, access test results and drug stocks. TRACnet also helps central institutions to monitor epidemiology, manage drug supply chains, improve accountability, and incentivize local institutions.

Strong adoption rates have been reported. Coverage for patients eligible for ART went up from 13 percent in 2005 to 79 percent in 2010. By 2011, nearly all the country's health centers had adopted TRACnet, including all of those providing ART. About 1200 health workers and more than 100,000 registered patients were benefiting from the system.

As a next step, the implementing company, Voxiva, intends to expand TRACnet to monitor 19 more infections, including malaria, cholera, measles, and swine flu. Despite some evaluation problems, TRACnet has been considered a successful government-driven initiative, in which official health agencies collabo-rate with local clinics, donors, universities, and private companies.

8.2.4 One Laptop Per Child

The One Laptop Per Child initiative (OLPC), initiated around 2005, aims to make low-cost basic computers available to children in developing countries. Its global impact is contested,[1] but the Government of Rwanda and President

Kagame have frequently reiterated their support. Trials started in Rwanda in 2007, followed by distribution of a reported 80,000 computers and deployment of 60,000 computers by 2012. An additional shipment of 100,000 devices was scheduled for summer 2012, set to cover schools in all of the country's administrative sectors. About 1,500 teachers have been trained to work with students using the laptop, with another 1,200 to follow.

Despite positive results from early, small-scale evaluations,[2] the project has faced considerable problems. The unit cost of $181 is high in relation to available expenditure for education as a whole. Many schools lack electricity and laptops cannot usually be taken to students' homes, as the risk that they will be lost, stolen, or sold is thought too high.

Comprehensive evaluation of the OLPC project in Rwanda has yet to be carried out. For now, the government is committed to providing students with hands-on technology experience during primary education. It believes that early exposure to computers leads to rapid self-learning and that, complemented by training, the laptops will help students to build their ICT capacities and be more productive. Children receiving a laptop are reported to be enthusiastic, and some results show that they may learn to use their laptops faster than their teachers.

8.3 Distinctive Factors of Rwanda's ICT Experience

8.3.1 Leadership Commitment

Many observers have noted the importance of leadership from the top of government to the progress made by Rwanda's ICT sector. President Kagame has repeatedly highlighted the role of ICTs and skills development. His government has given ICTs a central role in national development policy within *Vision 2020*. The Ministry of Science, Technology and Scientific Research, together with RURA, RITA, and NITC, has received substantial political support and resources to encourage reforms and facilitate ICT deployment.

One thing that differentiates Rwanda's experience from many others is that ICTs have always been considered an explicit tool for development. ICTs have not been seen as an incidental set of technologies, secondary to traditional economic sectors where employment opportunities are concerned, but as a critical strategic driver of economic growth for a country with few alternative development strategies.

8.3.2 International Engagement

Private investment and funds from international donors have provided the financial backbone for project implementation. Many of Rwanda's ICT initiatives—such as improvements in the nationwide fiber backbone and training to tackle skill shortages—have been undertaken at substantial scale. This has been made possible by large commitments from bilateral and multilateral donors, including the World Bank, partly the result of Rwanda's high profile following the 1994 genocide and civil war. The World Bank's Regional Communications Infrastructure Programme (RCIP), for example, has contributed $24 million to support e-government and telecommunication infrastructure, integrating the national backbone with regional infrastructure and connecting it to East Africa's submarine cables.

Rwanda's aid dependency has reduced recently, but remains high in absolute terms: in 2011, about 40 percent of the nation's budget (or 11 percent of GDP) was financed by grants.[3] This presents significant risks. Several infrastructure projects were already facing unexpected funding shortages before recent reductions in aid by some donors following a United Nations report alleging Rwandese involvement in conflict in the Democratic Republic of Congo.[4]

8.3.3 Skills Development

A third distinctive factor of Rwanda's ICT-led development approach has been its strong emphasis on skills and training. *Vision 2020* recognized that while modernizing agriculture could enhance short to medium term economic growth, it would not eliminate structural challenges posed by weak institutions and a poorly educated workforce. Rwanda's policy makers saw the development of human resources as essential for it to make rapid progress out of poverty.

The Kigali Institute of Science, Technology and Management (KIST) has contributed to this approach, focusing on technology rather than a general course portfolio. Its mission is threefold: to develop skilled manpower, create and disseminate research, and deliver technical assistance and ICT training to the population. By 2002, KIST was able to cover 35 percent of its budget from entrepreneurial activities such as technology transfer projects, product development, and the KIST ICT Service Centre. Between 2001 and 2011, it has averaged around 2,700 students, with 750 graduating in 2012. Recently, it added an ICT e-learning facility to its portfolio.

Nevertheless, efforts to tackle the underlying shortage of ICT skills have not matched ambitious goals declared in *Vision 2020* and NICI plans. Diffusion of ICTs in education, fueled through large investments of donors and NGOs including OLPC, has risen dramatically throughout the mid-2000s. Turning this into skills development across the population has been more challenging. Researchers have found that the devices and resources available do not reach girls and marginalized communities in rural areas as well as they might, and that distance learning for teachers has proved more difficult than had been expected. In spite of the government's emphasis on ICTs, limited awareness of their potential is still believed to hinder adoption in rural communities.

8.3.4 Private Sector Development

Although the Government of Rwanda has played a very active role in the country's ICT development strategy, including infrastructure deployment, its stated aim has been to enable private sector transformation. As *Vision 2020* puts it, "the Government of Rwanda will not be involved in providing services and products that can be delivered more efficiently by the private sector, [...] [T]he State will only act as a catalyst."[5] While President Kagame's administration has sought to develop a policy environment which is favorable for the private sector, investment remains stubbornly low (10.9 percent of GDP in 2010, compared to 14.4 percent in the Sub-Saharan region).[6] Mostly, this is blamed on the lack of a skilled labor force, reinforcing the need for investment in education and skills training described above.

Supporting sustainable private sector development is as much a long-term endeavor as transforming skills and human capacity. The private sector in Rwanda consists mostly of a small-scale informal economy and suffers from a lack of basic infrastructure. ICT entrepreneurs find it difficult to grow new businesses in this environment. While the government's expansionary policy has helped the private ICT sector to some degree, it will take time for it to thrive and make a substantial contribution to national economic output.

Rwanda therefore has to walk a fine line between using government money and services to promote quick developmental gains in ICTs, and relying on a weaker private sector to achieve this. For example, KIST's ICT Centre—a government-subsidized entity—acts as an Internet service provider (ISP), offering a valued service to consumers but competing with private sector ISPs. Privatization and liberalization of the mobile operator market have also had variable results: MTN's monopoly only ended in 2006 and it took three more years until a third operator entered the market. The report suggests that it may be time for the government to shift gears in private sector development, fostering public-private partnerships to enhance entrepreneurship and private sector growth while scaling down support from public funds. A downturn in donor support may push the government in this direction.

8.4 Conclusion

Development does not come quickly, but Rwanda has made considerable progress since the 1994 genocide and civil war. A strong government has pursued a bold agenda for prosperity, with a clear emphasis on ICT as a critical driver. Putting ICT at the core of its development approach has distinguished Rwanda from many other countries. There are few such strong examples of policy makers' determination to turn their country into a regional and worldwide ICT hub.

There are now some results to show from this. Mobile subscriptions have grown very rapidly, though this is generally the case in Africa; 3G networks have begun to be deployed; and consumer prices for communications are likely to fall further with improving infrastructure and bandwidth. Large scale software applications have been deployed with some demonstrable development impact, for instance, in e-government and m-health.

Overall, this experience has derived from choice of development strategy, rather than being explicitly associated with efforts at postconflict reconstruction. The extent to which development and reconstruction strategies are intertwined is discussed in Part 1 of the report.

Ongoing challenges in Rwanda include issues of structural and cultural change. People are still not as aware of the benefits of ICTs as the government envisaged. Human resources, including ICT skills, have not yet been improved sufficiently to generate a highly skilled labor force. Increasing Internet access and the number of devices in the country has not delivered as many developmental gains as were anticipated, and there have been significant problems in implementing NICI plans. The fledgling private sector has not yet nearly grown enough to make government and donor funding unnecessary. The development of competitive ICT sectors in neighboring countries will also challenge some of the government's aims to make Rwanda an ICT hub within its region. Nevertheless, Rwanda provides a valuable case study, illustrating both what is possible in the tumult of postconflict situations and the difficulties of coordinating and enabling widespread economic and social transformation.

Notes

1. K. Kraemer, J. Dedrick, and P. Sharma (2009), "One Laptop per Child: Vision vs. Reality," *Communications of the ACM* 52, no. 6: 66–73.

2. http://wiki.laptop.org/images/a/a5/OLPC_Lit_Review_v4_Aug2010.pdf.

3. http://go.worldbank.org/YP79K5BDT0.

4. http://www.trademarksa.org/news/key-projects-rwanda-delayed-investors-cut-back-funding.

5. http://www.gesci.org/assets/files/Rwanda_Vision_2020.pdf.

6. http://web.worldbank.org/WBSITE/EXTERNAL/COUNTRIES/AFRICAEXT/RWANDAEXTN/0,,menuPK:368714~pagePK:141132~piPK:141107~theSitePK:368651,00.html.

The Role of Information and Communication Technologies in Postconflict Reconstruction
http://dx.doi.org/10.1596/978-1-4648-0074-0

CHAPTER 9

Timor-Leste

Timor-Leste (East Timor) is one of the world's newest independent states. Briefly independent after decolonization by Portugal in 1975, it was forcibly incorporated into its neighbor Indonesia the following year, leading to more than 20 years of armed conflict that cost over 100,000 lives, perhaps more than twice that number. A large majority of East Timorese rejected incorporation in Indonesia, effectively voting in favor of independence, in a referendum organized by the United Nations in 1999, an outcome which was followed by further violent conflict that left more than 1,000 dead, 300,000 in exile, and much of the country's infrastructure destroyed. It took three more years to restore normality before Timor-Leste was recognized as an independent state in 2002. Even then, internal tensions led to renewed political violence in 2006, and to further United Nations intervention. Apart from an unsuccessful rebel attack on the country's political leadership in 2008, it has remained at peace since then.

Violence and underdevelopment have left Timor-Leste economically weak, politically fractured, and highly dependent on international donors, though it has seen considerable rebuilding over the past decade. Its population of just over a million has been growing as refugees return, but human resources and skills are limited. Literacy is low and education weak. Surrounded by powerful neighbors (Indonesia and Australia), with weak political and economic institutions, it initially struggled to build sustainable economic growth. The advent of oil and gas exploitation, however, has had a major impact on its economic outlook, with revenues of over US$20 billion expected to accrue to Timor-Leste from just the Greater Sunrise field in the Timor Sea. As other oil-rich LDCs have found, integrating these revenues into national development without undermining other economic sectors can be highly problematic.

This chapter begins by describing the development and current status of the information and communication technology (ICT) sector in Timor-Leste. It then considers the role which ICTs have played in three main areas of postconflict reconstruction: in reconciliation, governance, and human development. The chapter concludes with reflections on the way forward.

9.1 ICTs in Timor-Leste

The history of telecommunications in Timor-Leste is brief. The country's entire preindependence telecoms infrastructure was destroyed during the conflict of 1999, along with its electricity grid. Today's telecoms networks and services have been put in place since then with private sector investment and international funding.

For most of the period since independence, Timor Telecom, which is majority owned by Portugal Telecom, has enjoyed a monopoly in telecoms service provision. Competition was only introduced in 2012 with the award of two new GSM/3G licences. Services are almost entirely mobile and the country has shared the worldwide experience of rapid growth in the number of mobile users. By the end of 2012, mobile service coverage extended to 92.5 percent of the population and Timor Telecom had just over 620,000 subscribers, a teledensity of around 55 percent. There were, however, only around 3,000 fixed lines in the country, and only 600 fixed broadband connections.

The Internet is still in its infancy in Timor-Leste. At the end of 2011, there were just 4,456 mobile and 1,068 fixed Internet connections in the country, equivalent to less than 0.5 percent of the population—and many of these lines belonged to expatriates and international agencies. There was only one Internet Service Provider (ISP) in competition with Timor Telecom, and there was little in the way of local content. Lack of international submarine cable connectivity means that bandwidth is low and usage costs are high. Local citizens are much likelier to use cybercafés than to have personal access to the Internet.

The regulatory framework for telecommunications is changing. Two government agencies have played key roles in recent years—the Department of Infrastructure, established in 2007 to oversee all utility sectors, and the regulatory authority ARCOM (*Autoridade Reguladora das Communicações*), which was first established in 2003. ARCOM will be replaced by a new regulator, ANC (*Autoridade Nacional de Communicações*), under new legislation which was being enacted at the time of the study. ANC will have more independence than its predecessor, and will be funded from licence and other fees levied on telecoms operators. It will oversee a liberalized market, in which market forces rather than government policy should call the tune. A universal access fund, the Telecom Fund of Timor-Leste—funded by operator levies, donors, and government grants—will be able to subsidize coverage in unprofitable areas. World Bank support has been provided for this new policy and regulatory environment.

The National Telecommunications Policy, adopted in 2011, recognizes the limitations posed by the lack of international submarine connectivity and the need to explore opportunities for redressing this, but no negotiations or funding proposals were reported in the study. Reliance on satellite connectivity will continue to inhibit Internet use and the potential development of Internet-enabled businesses and services in the short to medium term. The country lacks the skills as well as connectivity to build a meaningful business process outsourcing (BPO) or ICT-enabled services (ITES) sector.

The Role of Information and Communication Technologies in Postconflict Reconstruction
http://dx.doi.org/10.1596/978-1-4648-0074-0

The most cost-effective option for unlocking international bandwidth in the short term would be to connect to cables that currently land in, or will shortly reach, Indonesian West Timor. More costly options would be to connect with cables reaching Australia or Singapore.

9.2 ICTs and Reconciliation

Timor-Leste's preindependence and postindependence conflicts have left it in need of reconciliation both across and within its borders. As the country's dominant neighbor, Indonesia remains critically important to its future. Sustainable political institutions need to be developed in the country. ICTs and media have some part to play in each of these.

An Indonesia-Timor-Leste Commission of Truth and Friendship—a truth and reconciliation commission along the lines of that in South Africa—was established in 2005, six years after the 1999 conflict (with which, alone, it was concerned) and only shortly before the internal conflict of 2006. Its report in 2008 led to a measure of reconciliation, and there is increasing economic cooperation between the two countries.

The role of media and ICTs in reconciliation is discussed in Part 1 of this report. In Timor-Leste, as in many poor postconflict societies, especially those with low populations, radio and other media have received financial and other support from international donors in the early years of reconstruction, but this donor support has proved difficult to sustain in the longer term, leaving nascent media outlets precarious or unsustainable.

State and community radio stations are the most widely accessed mass media in Timor-Leste. Television has limited reach, while newspaper circulation is limited not least by high levels of illiteracy. The number of radio stations is declining, with community radio in particular finding it difficult to survive. Of 15 stations set up during the transitional government period (1999–2002), only six remained active in 2006.

One consequence of the weakness of domestic broadcasting is the reach of Indonesian media, particularly satellite television and pop music, into Timor-Leste. Although Tetun and Portuguese are the country's official languages, Bahasa Indonesia is spoken and understood by 60 percent of the population, making content from the country's neighbor and former ruler more accessible.

The influence of this cultural cross-fertilization on reconciliation is unclear. The report suggests that more use could be made of Bahasa content, for example in education, though this may be politically sensitive. Some experience is reported in the ICT sector, where the UN's Asia-Pacific Training Centre for ICT has used Bahasa materials and Indonesian experts to train senior government officials.

9.3 ICTs and Governance

Like many postconflict societies, Timor-Leste was left after 1999 with very weak government institutions and public infrastructure. A transitional administration was provided by the United Nations from 1999 to 2002, and the country is still heavily reliant on the UN and international donors. The UN Development Programme (UNDP) cited ongoing problems of corruption and inefficiency in its 2011 National Human Development Report, and the country ranked 143rd of 183 countries in Transparency International's Corruption Perception Index for 2011. The advent of oil revenues offers positive economic prospects but also requires strong administration.

As discussed in the overview chapter, ICTs have potential for improving and strengthening institutions while also enhancing public participation in decision making. Some donor-funded projects have concentrated in this area. UNDP, for example, launched a programme to facilitate human resource management in government—the Personnel Management Information System (PMIS)—during 2007. It is now supporting ICT training of staff from the Ministry of Justice and other law enforcement agencies, including training of trainers which, it is hoped, will make these departments more independent of external aid in future.

The challenge of integrating technology with governance is considerable. The viability of UNDP's PMIS initiative is undermined by lack of connectivity between government departments and limited use of email by officials. Government departments have adopted different standards for hardware and software, making integration difficult to achieve. Many officials, including war veterans, lack necessary skills.

Even the technology itself is problematic. ICT hardware has to be imported, and there are few people with the skills required to maintain equipment. The use of Portuguese as an official language poses software challenges, though it has also encouraged adoption of open source programmes, pioneered by an Australian government supported project, Info Exchange East Timor, and by the Department of Justice. Salaries for ICT professionals in the private sector and development agencies are around twice those in government departments, making it difficult for the latter to retain skilled staff.

There is, finally, no established culture of public information and consultation in Timor-Leste, making it hard to enable public participation in decision making. A web portal, www.transparency.gov.tl, was launched by the Ministry of Finance in March 2011, enabling citizens to search, evaluate, and analyse state spending. This includes an e-procurement subportal. Increased transparency will, it is hoped, reduce corruption. However, issues of language, connectivity/access, and poor citizen skills limit meaningful public access to this portal to such an extent that the study authors felt it cannot currently achieve these objectives.

9.4 ICTs and Human Development

Timor-Leste has long been one of Asia's poorest and least developed countries. Recent years, however, have seen substantial economic growth. Gross domestic product (GDP) p.c. has risen from $300 to $800 since independence, with annual growth rates approaching 8 percent.

This growth resulted initially from the injection of donor funding in an economy left at a low ebb by prolonged conflict. The crucial turning point since independence, however, came in 2004 when oil extraction began in the Timor Sea. Since then, the country has become heavily oil dependent. By 2009, petroleum accounted for about 95 percent of total government revenue and almost 80 percent of gross national income. While positive in many ways, this also poses challenges. A highly dominant oil extraction industry can drain resources from other sectors, while there is no guarantee that oil revenues will be used for human development. In Timor-Leste, the government has established a Petroleum Fund, with assets of almost US$10 billion by early 2012, to develop infrastructure and human resources.

Other economic sectors—agriculture (including coffee, the major export in the colonial period but neglected since the 1970s), industry, and services—are now dwarfed by the oil economy. Although some Internet marketing of Timorese coffee is mentioned, the study does not identify specific ways in which ICTs are contributing to these other economic sectors. International experience suggests that there is potential for them to make a contribution, even for low-income subsistence farmers, not least in supply chain management.

The positive figures for economic growth described above have not yet been reflected in human development outcomes. Timor-Leste still has one of the lowest rankings in UNDP's Human Development Index—147th out of 187 countries in 2011. It is unlikely to achieve about half of the UN's Millennium Development Goals by 2015. So far, oil revenue has not trickled down to the poor and 41 percent of the population lives below the national poverty line, with a sharp increase in urban poverty occurring during the first decade of the century.

UNDP believes that it is critical for the country to identify ways both to pass on the benefits of the oil economy to the poor and to develop and diversify the nonoil economy, especially in rural areas. The lack of relevant human skills means that BPO and ITES sectors, which are being promoted in a number of developing countries, are not viable options in Timor-Leste. One area which is suggested by the report, in which ICTs could be of value, is international tourism, where its authors feel the experience of Maldives may be valuable—though there are also very substantial differences between the two countries which must be considered. Maldives has a well-established high-end tourism industry, with a reputation for quality and strong links with major international tourism businesses.

Perhaps the most difficult national development challenge lies in education. The Fundamental Schools Quality Project (2002–06) invested $20 million in primary education, and the World Bank has supported ongoing educational improvements. The current Education Sector Support Programme is investing a further $6 million in improving education management. One particular challenge in education is an historic gap in education and literacy between boys and girls.

Almost no attention has been paid to date to ICT education. Few tertiary colleges offer ICT courses and these have difficulty finding lecturers or developing ICT facilities. The Global Development Learning Network of the World Bank Institute has a node in the capital, Dili, which provides some expertise and training with a particular focus on public administration. However, most of its courses are in English and there is little demand for advanced courses.

The Role of Information and Communication Technologies in Postconflict Reconstruction
http://dx.doi.org/10.1596/978-1-4648-0074-0

With current resource constraints at school level, the study argues, it would be better to focus ICT education on secondary than primary schools. Other opportunities for ICT learning include internationally accepted certificates such as those provided by Cisco and other companies. Employers often face difficulties in recruiting staff with skills in software usage, though the report notes that this, and partnerships between Timor-Leste and Brazil, may encourage the use of open source applications. In the longer term, the study notes the need to develop higher-level ICT skills within the local market, including graphics applications, web development, and programming.

Alongside education, health is often identified as a crucial development sector for the use of ICTs. The World Health Organization strongly advocates improving communication systems to reduce health risks and has proposed several ICT-enabled initiatives in its Country Cooperation Strategy for 2009–13. These include the use of geographic information systems (GIS) to collect health data and manage both diseases and emergencies. Specialized training of health professionals in data management and GIS applications will be needed for this to succeed.

Population pressures, unregulated development and deforestation have degraded Timor's environment in recent years. The study identified no current environmental applications using ICTs in the country, but noted that GIS applications are increasingly used in other countries including island states such as the Republic of the Maldives.

9.5 The Way Forward

Timor-Leste faces deep-seated problems of development which have been exacerbated by years of conflict associated with the national struggle for independence. While the country's international status was resolved following the 1999 referendum and subsequent international intervention, political institutions remain weak and the country's continued vulnerability led to an outbreak of civil strife in 2006. Oil revenues are now contributing to national wealth, but the impact of this is not yet being felt significantly in social development outcomes.

The liberalization of Timor-Leste's telecommunications sector, which is still underway, should lead to further reductions in prices, improvements in service, and the development of a "mobile culture" of the kind that has emerged in other Asian countries. The broadening of access to communications services and applications should help to engage citizens more effectively in their society.

For the potential of broadband to be realized, however, Timor-Leste needs to gain access to international fiber networks rather than continuing to rely on satellite connectivity. Achieving this should be a priority for the new regulator ANC. The most likely source of submarine connectivity lies in accessing cables that currently reach or will shortly reach Indonesian West Timor, which may also facilitate reconciliation.

Development areas in which ICTs can play a useful role include education (especially distance learning), healthcare, agriculture, and tourism. ICTs can also play an important part in public administration, not least in enabling transparency and tackling corruption. Development partners can make a contribution to this.

As in other countries emerging from conflict and embracing new opportunities, the role of ICTs in Timor-Leste's political and economic development is complex. New media, including social media, can have a significant effect on social and political relationships, both within the country and between Timor-Leste and Indonesia. These could foster reconciliation but could also be less constructive. Access to ICTs is limited by lack of human capacity and educational attainment, but ICTs also offer opportunities to redress educational imbalances and weaknesses. The increasing dominance of oil in the Timorese economy has not diminished the need for diversification and development in other economic sectors that can generate employment. Even without government intervention, as ICTs become more widely available they are likely to play a more significant part in national social, political, and economic change. The potential and challenges arising from this are discussed in Part 1 of the report.

CHAPTER 10

Tunisia

Tunisia's experience, as the first country in its region to change governments in what has become known as the Arab Spring, has made it the focus of media and policy debate about large-scale changes taking place in world society, including those associated with information and communication technologies (ICTs), the Internet, and social networking. Some have argued that Tunisia and other countries in the throes of political change have demonstrated the power of informed and networked individuals to challenge established rulers and social structures. Others have seen the role of information and communications media as more instrumental, offering citizens new ways of organizing and gathering opinion, circumventing government surveillance and building alliances between groups in ways that were not previously available. Others again point out that popular unrest leading to governmental change is nothing new: insurrections in the past took place in the absence of Facebook and Twitter, they argue, and new media merely offer new ways of channelling old politics.

The study of Tunisia undertaken for this World Bank programme does not seek to explore these issues comprehensively but to make a contribution to understanding of them within the complexities of Tunisian society, economy, and culture. Using an ethnographic approach, it draws on 100 interviews with Tunisians of varying backgrounds and experience, undertaken after the departure of former president Ben Ali in 2011, to consider three questions:

- How can critical social, civil, and governmental institutions use ICTs to improve organizational efficiency, public engagement, service delivery, and overall accountability?
- How should policy makers and investors structure and prioritize technology initiatives to spur economic development and technological innovation?
- How can the use of ICTs among citizens, media, and civic institutions encourage social cohesion and build social resilience?

The study develops an analysis of Tunisia's society and recent history to provide a basis for conclusions which add to the diverse range of views about the country, its political direction, and the role of ICTs which can be found in current media and other literature. At the heart of its assessment lies a perception of the role of connectedness in challenging the old regime. "Connectivity," the authors argue, "expanded awareness of economic inequality and increased levels of popular frustration; it also strengthened citizens' ability to organize and demonstrate." While citizens took advantage of this new connectedness, the governing elite did not: "the structures, tools, and processes of governance adapted to new ICTs slowly, and with difficulty." As a result, the study argues, Tunisia offered to its region and the world an example of what could happen when citizens exercise the power of connectivity and demand recognition of their rights.

Five themes emerge from this analysis. Together, these themes explore the role and impact of communications in the context of underlying issues in the recent development of Tunisia (before, during, and since its change of government), review the potential of communications in the country's ongoing political and economic development, and consider its significance for citizen empowerment and social change. The five themes are concerned with:

- The need to address regional disparity, seen as a challenge from the country's past but also an opportunity for its future
- The role of small and medium-sized enterprises (SMEs) in building an entrepreneurial economy
- The need for investment in more appropriate higher education
- The potential of participatory politics
- The emergence of new kinds of civil society, increasingly driven by online connectivity.

10.1 Addressing Regional Disparity

The first of these five themes emphasizes differences between communities within Tunisia, their opportunities and aspirations. Interior provinces of the country have been isolated from its coastal hubs by distance and poor transport and information networks, and have as a result been much more economically distressed. Regional disparity contributed toward a general hostility to government before and during the uprising in 2011. Efforts to address economic disparity now may also improve government accountability and inclusiveness, but it will be difficult to erase the impact of long years of disadvantage. Although people appear to understand that change will take time, they also need to see signs that change is happening. Unrest in the provinces could continue if there is no improvement, undermining the authority of the elected government.

These challenges are illustrated by experience in a representative provincial town, Thala, in the western central area of the country. Resources there remain deficient after the revolution, as they were before. There is limited employment and there are few economic opportunities. Farmers lack the capital for irrigation which could increase their productivity and income levels. Medical facilities are much inferior to those in coastal areas. Fewer people have mobile phones and there is no Internet connectivity.

Trust in institutions in such communities is low. Local leadership is weak and there is residual distrust of the police following events during the uprising. The evidence presented in the study suggests that improved transport and digital connectivity could play an important part in overcoming disadvantage, though this requires more than simply deploying new technology: the mechanisms by which the benefits of technology are diffused and integrated into everyday life, at local level, will also be crucial.

A vital question in Thala and many similar areas, therefore, concerns the extent to which the new regime will address their disadvantage, encouraging greater social and geographical inclusion. "For people living at subsistence levels," the report concludes, "there is the sense that things could change drastically against their favor in an instant. Yet, they believe that the current postrevolutionary political opening offers their first chance to change existing power structures in decades. This understandably has those living in marginalized communities aggressively advocating for their needs while they feel the door is open."

10.2 The Role of SMEs

The second theme of the report emphasizes the role of small and medium-sized enterprises. As in many middle- and lower-income countries, these provide the majority of employment and have the potential to grow rapidly in the right conditions, if they have the freedom to innovate and reach out to new markets. While many small enterprises are in traditional sectors such as farming, technology, including ICTs, offers new entrepreneurial opportunities for SMEs. Their dynamism, it is suggested, could in turn attract investment into the country from multinational firms.

Tunisia's old regime, the report argues, sought to control innovation, fearful of its impact on social change, though it did invest substantial resources in higher education concerned with computer science and engineering, so the country does have quite a high level of ICT expertise and ICT business activity. By unleashing innovation, it is suggested that the new government could dynamize the economy—encouraging local entrepreneurs to remain in-country, those in the diaspora to return, and those in the interior to believe that they have opportunities that are worth pursuing.

The new government, the report suggests, could take a number of initiatives to promote ICT entrepreneurship along these lines—for example, by liberalizing the use of data derived from geographic information system (GIS) and other sources, by enabling a more effective online customer payment gateway than is currently available in Tunisia, by increasing competition in procurement, and by supporting the establishment of incubators and technoparks. While the previous government did invest in incubators, these have so far struggled to achieve results. A new approach to them could be much more productive.

The Role of Information and Communication Technologies in Postconflict Reconstruction
http://dx.doi.org/10.1596/978-1-4648-0074-0

10.3 Investment in Higher Education

The report's third theme concerns higher education. Although Tunisia has had a substantial higher education sector, with a high proportion of graduates, the report argues that curricula have been ill-suited to the country's needs, emphasizing theoretical rather than practical knowledge (even in areas such a tourism and business studies) and focused on equipping students for employment in established economic sectors which cannot easily absorb more people.

Three specific problems are identified in the established education system. Access to educational opportunities has depended not so much on school performance as on family background and geographical location. Students have usually attended universities near to their home areas, exacerbating disparities between coastal hubs, which have better universities, and the interior. Few universities, it is noted, have benefited from participation in the national research and education network, even though this was initiated as long ago as 1997.

Tunisia has invested heavily in higher education over the years, and education is highly valued by the young, but this investment has not been well attuned to national needs. Organizational capacity has been limited by poor technology and a lack of rigor in evaluating educational outcomes. Universities' training capacity needs to be upgraded so that students graduate more practically equipped to contribute to national development. A number of measures could be taken to address these challenges—including an emphasis on applied education, not least in ICT skills; learning from the private sector; building stronger links between educational institutions and technoparks; and addressing regional disparities in educational opportunity. There is also scope for more distance learning in the future educational portfolio.

10.4 Participatory Politics

One of the most obvious changes brought about by the uprising in 2011 lies at the heart of the report's fourth theme—the development of a more inclusive and participatory political marketplace. Political participation was effectively denied to ordinary citizens before the revolution. Since, there has been an enormous and unstructured increase in what citizens can do. Many people have enthusiastically taken up new political opportunities, encouraged by this and by free and fair elections.

The consequences are not, however, as simple as they seem. Generations of authoritarian rule have left people struggling with the mechanisms of popular participation. "The explosion of new information and media," the report's authors argue, "is confounding the efforts of new voters who are looking for reliable, easy-to-use sources of reliable political intelligence." There is an enormous range of new political parties and news sources from which to choose, from Facebook posts to blogs, television news to village "campaign walls" on which candidates presented information about themselves during recent elections. Tunisians lack experience in making informed choices about which information and which sources they can trust. The "signal-to-noise ratio," as the report puts it, "is out of balance."

New and emerging political leaders are trying to engage with the population but extremists are also exploiting the potential of new media opportunities. As well as representative political institutions, the country needs to develop and regularize participatory processes for political discourse and decision making. These may include informal institutions which have the capacity to stimulate more open dialogue. Two examples of these are included in the report:

• Zitouna radio station was once associated with the old regime, but has repositioned itself since the revolution as a forum for debate and transparency—respected, though unpopular with those who hold entrenched political positions.
• TEDx is a grassroots structure for facilitating debate through organized events which have proved attractive to younger, more affluent, technically aware Tunisians who are interested in stimulating business innovation and exploring new ideas.

Different fora, of which these are examples, will attract people from different backgrounds and with different perspectives. It is important that the development of open dialogue is inclusive of this diversity.

10.5 The Development of Civil Society

The report's fifth theme is the need for Tunisia to develop a vibrant and robust civil society, something that was suppressed under the old regime.

A good deal of civic activity is now taking place online. Indeed, the report suggests that "communities that have formed around digital tools and virtual spaces are rampant in Tunisia." Some of these have emerged from networks of ICT technicians which took advantage of online discussion during the revolution to open up non-technical debates. Others have been built within global applications such as Facebook (in particular), YouTube, and instant messaging services. During the revolution, these online networks served as a grapevine through which news of events spread throughout the population. These developments should be crucial in the future to engaging an increasingly connected populace.

The extent to which the Internet is available is still, however, something of a constraint. Internet usage was estimated at just over 36 percent of the population in January 2012, higher in the coastal belt than the interior. About 20 percent of Tunisians were said to be on Facebook. Contrary to some published comment, Twitter was not widely used in Tunisia at the time of the uprising. Mobile services have much greater reach, with teledensity of 85 percent.

The report sees great potential in the future development of online communities, not just in social and political activity but also in building entrepreneurship and economic opportunity. However, networked activists have not yet found their place within the changing institutions of government. "The fate of these

The Role of Information and Communication Technologies in Postconflict Reconstruction
http://dx.doi.org/10.1596/978-1-4648-0074-0

communities of bloggers, hackers, and engineers is uncertain," says the report; "their path from organic online networks to a position of substantial influence in real world politics is uncharted." The next year should make that future much more clear.

10.6 Building a Twenty-First-Century Social Compact

The study of Tunisia described in this chapter is concerned with the relationship between communications and society in a particular context—one in which authoritarianism has historically constrained opportunity, expression, and entrepreneurship, and in which people are attempting, with a good deal of uncertainty as well as optimism, to transcend that legacy. The challenges described in the report—challenges such as regional disparity, weak entrepreneurial capacity, and misplaced educational priorities—cannot be transformed by communications alone. They are dependent on larger changes in political, economic, and social order, whose outcomes are far from certain. Communications do, however, have a powerful potential impact on the ways in which political, economic, and social order can evolve, offering new channels for citizens to engage with their society, create, and take advantage of opportunities.

Social and political developments in countries which have undergone major change following insurrection are often rapid and unpredictable. This has certainly been the case in Tunisia, whose political evolution since the overthrow of the Ben Ali regime has been complex and turbulent. The trends discussed in this study form an important part of the environment in which these social and political developments are taking place. The relationship between them and other factors influencing social and political change will vary over time and should be reassessed as the situation in Tunisia develops further.

At the time that the research was undertaken, its authors concluded that Tunisia's experience had demonstrated the potential of ICTs to advance participatory politics—"the public square," as they call it. Technology, they argue, has given the marginalized a greater awareness of regional, social, and political disparity, building political consciousness which can reach out beyond network originators to a much wider audience. Their report anticipates that continuing developments in information and communication technologies, and the uses to which they are put by politically conscious and connected networks, will increasingly challenge policy makers, political leaders, and other influential stakeholders. This, they suggest, is "democratic policy-making for a democratic age." For this and other reasons, ICTs should play an important part in the reconstruction of Tunisian society following the uprising that overturned its long-standing authoritarian regime.

Selected Bibliography

Allen, Tim, and Nicole Stremlau. 2005. "Media Policy, Peace and State Reconstruction." Discussion Paper no. 8, London School of Economics Crisis States Research Centre .

Aron, Janine. 2003. "Building Institutions in Post-Conflict African Economies." *Journal of International Development* 15: 471–85.

BBC Media Action. 2012. *The Media of Afghanistan: The Challenges of Transition.*

Bott, Maja, and Young Gregor. 2011. "The Role of Crowdsourcing for Better Governance in Fragile State Contexts." World Bank, Washington, DC.

Bray, John. 2005. "*International Companies and Post-Conflict Reconstruction.*" World Bank Social Development Papers in Conflict Prevention and Reconstruction, no. 22.

Brod, Cesar. 2013. "The Promise of Open Data in Brazil: Fostering Participation, Building Open Communities." UNDP. https://www.undpegov.org/sites/undpegov.org/files/Brazil-OD-2013-05-29.pdf. .

Collier, Paul. 2003. "Breaking the Conflict Trap: Civil War and Development Policy," World Bank Policy Research Report, World Bank, Washington, DC.

———. 2004. "Development and Conflict." Oxford University Centre for the Study of African Economies, Oxford.

———. 2010. *Conflict, Political Accountability and Aid.* Routledge.

Coyle, Diane, and Patrick Meier. n.d. "New Technologies in Emergencies and Conflicts: The Role of Information and Social Networks." United Nations Foundation & Vodafone Foundation.

Cuttor, Ana. 2005. "Peace building: A literature review." *Development in Practice* 15 (6): 778–84.

Fearon, James D., Macartan Humphreys, and Jeremy M. Weinstein.2009. "Can Development Aid Contribute to Social Cohesion after Civil War? Evidence from a Field Experiment in Post-Conflict Liberia." *American Economic Review: Papers and Proceedings* 99 (2): 287–91.

ICT for Peace Foundation. 2010. "Cross-Fertilisation of UN Common Operational Datasets and Crisis Mapping." http://ict4peace.org/wp-content/uploads/2010/10/UN-and-CrisisMapping.pdf.

Kalathil, Shanthi. 2008. "Towards a New Model: Media and Communications in Post-Conflict and Fragile States." World Bank Communication for Governance and Accountability Program.

Kaltenborn-Stachau, Henriette von. 2008. "The Missing Link: Fostering Positive Citizen-state Relations in Post-conflict Environments." World Bank Communication for Governance and Accountability Program.

Konkel, Agnieszka, and Richard Heeks. 2008. "Challenging Conventional Views on Mobile Telecommunications Investment: Evidence from Conflict Zones." Development Informatics Short Paper no. 9, University of Manchester Development Informatics Group.

Krause, Keith, and Oliver Jütersonke. 2005. "Peace, Security and Development in Post-Conflict Environments." *Security Dialogue* 36 (4): 447–62.

Kreimer, Alcira et al. 1998. "The World Bank's Experience with Post-Conflict Reconstruction." World Bank Operations Evaluation Department.

Mancini, Francesco, ed. 2013. "New Technology and the Prevention of Violence and Conflict." United Nations Development Programme, USAID & International Peace Institute.

Melhem, Samia, Claudia Morrell, and Nidhi Tandon. 2007. "ICTs for Women's Socioeconomic Empowerment." World Bank. http://imagebank.worldbank.org/serv-let/WDSContentServer/IW3P/IB/2010/01/04/000333038_20100104233421/Rendered/PDF/518310PUB0REPL101Official0Use0Only1.pdf.

Milliken, Jennifer, and Keith Krause. 2002. "State Failure, State Collapse and State Reconstruction: Concepts, lessons and strategies." *Development and Change* 33 (5): 753–74.

Mills, Rob, and Qimiao Fan. 2006. "The Investment Climate in Post-Conflict Situations." World Bank Institute Investment Climate Capacity Enhancement Program, WPS4055.

Nathan, Laurie 2005. "'The Frightful Inadequacy of Most of the Statistics': A Critique of Collier and Hoeffler on Causes of Civil War." Crisis States Discussion Paper no. 11, London School of Economics & Political Science, Crisis States Development Research Centre.

Newman, Edward, Roland Paris, and Oliver P. Richmond. 2010. *New Perspectives on Liberal Peacebuilding*. New York: United Nations University.

Nooruddin, Irfan, and Thomas E. Flores. 2007. "Evaluating World Bank Post-Conflict Assistance Programs." Paper prepared for the 65th meeting of the Midwest Political Science Association, Chicago, Illinois.

Organisation for Economic Cooperation and Development, Development Assistance Committee. 2001. "Helping Prevent Violent Conflict: The DAC Guidelines." OECD.

Paris, Roland. 2004. *At War's End: BuildingPeace after Civil Conflict*. New York: Cambridge University Press.

Paris, Roland, and Timothy D. Sisk. 2008. *The Dilemmas of Statebuilding: Confronting the Contradictions of Postwar Peace Operations*. London and New York: Routledge.

Putzel, James, and Jonathan Di John. 2012. "Meeting the Challenges of Crisis States." London School of Economics & Political Science, Crisis States Development Research Centre.

Putzel, James, and Joost van der Zwan. 2005. "Why Templates for Media Development Do Not Work in Crisis States: Defining and Understanding Media Development Strategies in Post-war and Crisis States." London School of Economics & Political Science, Crisis States Development Research Centre.

Schwartz, Jordan, Shelly Hahn, and Ian Bannon. 2004. "The Private Sector's Role in the Provision of Infrastructure in Post-Conflict Countries: Patterns and Policy Options." World Bank Social Development Papers in Conflict Prevention and Reconstruction, no. 16.

Search for Common Ground. n.d. "Communication for Peacebuilding: Practices, Trends and Challenges." Support for Common Ground & United States Institute for Peace.

Sigal, Ivan. 2009. "Digital Media in Conflict-Prone Societies." National Endowment for Democracy Center for International Media Assistance.

Smith, Dan. 2004. "Towards a Strategic Framework for Peacebuilding: Getting Their Act Together—Overview Report of the Joint Utstein Study of Peacebuilding." Royal Norwegian Ministry of Foreign Affairs.

Smyth, Thomas N., John Etherton, and Michael L. Best. 2010. "MOSES: Exploring New Ground in Media and Post-conflict Reconstruction." Georgia Institute of Technology.

Stauffacher, Daniel, et al., eds. 2011. "Peacebuilding in the Information Age: Sifting Hype from Reality." ICT4Peace Foundation, Berkman Center for Internet and Society & Georgia Institute of Technology.

Stauffacher, Daniel, William Drake, Paul Currion, , and Julia Steinberger, . 2005. "Information and Communication Technology for Peace: The Role of ICT in Preventing, Responding to and Recovering from Conflict." United Nations ICT Task Force & ICT4Peace.

Stauffacher, Daniel, Sanjana Hattotuwa, and Barbara Weekes. 2012. "The Potential and Challenges of Open Data for Crisis Information Management and Aid Efficiency." ICT4Peace Foundation.

Teuten, Richard. 2007. "Stabilisation and "Post-Conflict" Reconstruction." Paper delivered at the Royal United Services Institute, London.

United Nations. 2009. "United Nations Policy for Post-Conflict Employment Creation, Income Generation and Reintegration." United Nations, Geneva.

United Nations Development Programme. 2012. "Mobile Technologies and Empowerment: Enhancing Human Development through Participation and Innovation." http://www.undpegov.org/sites/undpegov.org/files/undp_mobile_technology_primer.pdf.

United Nations Development Programme, World Bank & United Nations Development Group. 2004. "Practical Guide to Multilateral Needs Assessments in Post-Conflict Situations." Separate volume of "Supporting Material."

UNESCO. 2004. "Media Conflict Prevention and Reconstruction." UNESCO.

UNICEF. 2011. "The Role of Education in Peacebuilding: Literature Review." UNICEF.

USAID. 2009. "A Guide to Economic Growth in Post-Conflict Countries." USAID Office of Economic Growth.

Weekes, Barbara, and Eneken Tikk-Ringas. 2013. "Cybersecurity Affairs. Global and Regional Processes, Agendas and Instruments." ICT4Peace Foundation.

World Bank. 2011. "World Development Report 2011: Conflict, Security and Development." World Bank, Washington, DC.

———. 2012. ICT for Greater Development Impact: ICT Sector Strategy. World Bank, Washington, DC.

Environmental Benefits Statement

The World Bank is committed to reducing its environmental footprint. In support of this commitment, the Publishing and Knowledge Division leverages electronic publishing options and print-on-demand technology, which is located in regional hubs worldwide. Together, these initiatives enable print runs to be lowered and shipping distances decreased, resulting in reduced paper consumption, chemical use, greenhouse gas emissions, and waste.

The Publishing and Knowledge Division follows the recommended standards for paper use set by the Green Press Initiative. Whenever possible, books are printed on 50 percent to 100 percent postconsumer recycled paper, and at least 50 percent of the fiber in our book paper is either unbleached or bleached using Totally Chlorine Free (TCF), Processed Chlorine Free (PCF), or Enhanced Elemental Chlorine Free (EECF) processes.

More information about the Bank's environmental philosophy can be found at http://crinfo.worldbank.org/wbcrinfo/node/4.

The Role of Information and Communication Technologies in PostConflict Reconstruction
http://dx.doi.org/10.1596/978-1-4648-0074-0